THE GODS AND THEIR GRAND DESIGN

Also by Erich von Däniken

Chariots of the Gods
Return to the Stars
Gold of the Gods
In Search of Ancient Gods
Miracles of the Gods
According to the Evidence
Signs of the Gods
Pathways to the Gods

THE GODS
AND THEIR
GRAND DESIGN

The Eighth Wonder
of the World

by
ERICH VON DÄNIKEN

Translated by Michael Heron

G. P. Putnam's Sons
New York

First published in Germany 1982 under the title *Die Strategie
Der Götter*

Library of Congress Cataloging in Publication Data

Däniken, Erich von, 1935–
    The Gods and their grand design.

    Translation of: Strategie der Götter.
    1. Civilization, Ancient — Extraterrestrial influences.
    2. Indians of South America — Colombia — Antiquities.
    3. Colombia — Antiquities.   I. Title.
CB156.D35713   1984   001.9′4   83–27066
ISBN 0–399–12961–8

Printed in Great Britain

Contents

1 Legendary Times!

'We should not fear those who hold different opinions, but those who hold different opinions and are too cowardly to say so.'
Napoleon 1 (1769–1821)

Reality is more fantastic than any fantasy.

Before I can follow a trail that was laid many thousands of years ago, I must tell you about an astounding but controversial event that took place in America in the first third of the last century. It leads us back to that ancient trail.

Among the immigrants who streamed into the New World from Germany, Scandinavia, Ireland and England was the Smith family from Scotland, who lived in the small town of Palmyra in New York State.

The district in which the Smiths lived was still barely civilised. Day-to-day existence demanded hard physical toil from the immigrants. The American War of Independence from 1776 to 1783 already lay fifty years behind, but the vast country was still very sparsely inhabited and the settlers had to maintain running battles with the indigenous Indians.

The new arrivals from Europe were hard-working. Not only did they bring tools and goodwill with them, but also the many and varied religions of their homelands, which they sought to propagate with missionary zeal. Sects and religious groups spread like weeds. The apostles of salvation of countless different faiths vied with each other in making extravagant promises and capturing souls with sinister threats about the hereafter. Chapels, temples and churches shot up like mushrooms, as though the devil himself had discovered how to confuse the minds of the settlers in their new homeland.

Like many immigrants, Mother Smith and her three children were Presbyterians. Her son Joseph, who was eighteen, found things more difficult. He sought desperately for the true God, because he could not accept the fact that all the saviours claimed firmly to be in the right and at the same time fought each other bitterly in the name of Jesus. Joseph Smith (1805–1844) was a nonentity, until the night of 21 September 1823, when he had a strange vision.

Joseph was praying fervently in his bedroom, when he suddenly perceived a light, which illuminated the room brilliantly. A bare-footed angel in a white robe stepped out of the light. The vision introduced himself to the terrified youth as Moroni, the messenger of God. Moroni had astounding news for the young man!

The angel told him that in a stony hiding-place near the Smith family's home town a book was preserved written on gold plates and giving a full account of the former inhabitants

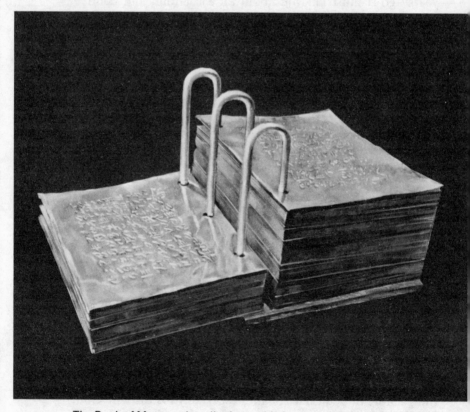

The Book of Mormon, inscribed on gold plates, revealed to Joseph Smith through a vision.

of the American continent and the source from whence they came. Near the gold tablets lay a breastplate to which two stones, Urim and Thummim,* were attached and with their help the ancient scripture could be translated. In addition the cache contained a divine compass. After telling Joseph Smith that he had been chosen to translate part of the scriptures and spread their message abroad, Moroni, the divine messenger, vanished.

Only for a while.

Then he reappeared, repeated the exciting news and added the prophecy that there would be great desolation by famine, sword and pestilence in the future.

We do not know whether Moroni was ordered to deliver his message bit by bit or whether he was forgetful. In any case he appeared for the third time on the night of 21 September to add a warning to his two previous messages. Joseph was forbidden to show the sacred objects on the Hill of Cumorah to anyone, apart from a chosen few. If he broke this commandment he would be killed.

Short of sleep after his nocturnal visit, Joseph naturally told his father about his alarming experience over their frugal breakfast. A bigoted believer like all the settlers, Father Smith had no doubt that his son had been given a divine mission — to seek out the place described by the angel Moroni.

South of Palmyra, near the village of Manchester, rises the Hill of Cumorah, which towers up steeply on its north side. Underneath the top of the hill Joseph Smith found the treasure he had been promised. This is how he himself described it:

Under a stone of considerable size lay the plates, deposited in a stone box. This stone was thicker and rounding in the middle on the upper side and thinner towards the edges, so that the middle part of it was visible above the ground, but the edge round was covered with earth. Having removed the earth, I obtained a lever, which I got fixed under the edge of the stone, and with a little exertion raised it up. I looked in, and there indeed did I behold the plates. The box in which they lay was formed by laying stones together in some kind of cement. In the bottom of the box were laid two stones

---

* Oracle stones used by the priests of Israel.

The Hill of Cumorah beneath whose summit Joseph Smith found the buried treasure, the plates of the Book of Mormon.

crossways of the box, and on these stones lay the plates and the other things with them.

When the teenager, with the curiosity of any treasure-hunter, automatically reached for the objects with both hands, he immediately felt a blow. He tried again and received another crippling blow. At the third attempt he received what seemed like a powerful electric shock. He lay on the floor as if paralysed.

At the same moment Moroni, the enigmatic nocturnal messenger, appeared beside him and ordered Joseph to return there every year on the same day. When the time was ripe, he would be given the sacred objects.

That time came four years later.

On 22 September 1827 the heavenly messenger Moroni handed Joseph Smith the engraved gold plates, the breastplate and the gleaming translation aids Urim and Thummim. Moroni impressed on the 22-year-old Joseph that he would be held responsible if the ancient treasures were lost owing to his carelessness.

I do not know if this story really took place like that. However that is exactly how it is handed down in *The Book of Mormon*, the 'Bible' of 'The Church of Jesus Christ of Latter-day Saints', the Mormons. It is the firm belief of several million Mormons, those devout people who have their headquarters in Salt Lake City in the State of Utah.

I do not know whether Joseph Smith was a religious psychopath or a crafty demagogue who took advantage of the religious confusion of his day to ensnare people. I do not know if Joseph Smith was a selfless, honourable truth-seeking prophet.

Nor do I know who visited the young man on the night of 21 September 1823 and handed over the hidden treasure four years later. Was it an Indian who knew of the existence of the ancient plates? Could he, or a member of his tribe, have hidden them? Did an Indian convert to one of the many Christian communities betray a well-preserved secret? Did a white treasure-hunter, who needed a partner, initiate Joseph Smith? Or did the young man stumble on the treasure trove alone and invent the story of the heavenly vision to attract attention?

I do not know the answer, but one thing seems certain. Joseph Smith actually possessed the engraved gold plates!

With the help of the 'translation stones' Urim and Thummim, Joseph Smith had worked for 21 months translating part of the text on the plates before he showed them to three honourable and respected men in June 1829 — with the angel Moroni's permission, of course! Oliver Cowdery, David Whitmer and Martin Harris drew up a document in which they swore that they had seen the plates 'and the engravings thereon'.

This testimony carries some weight, for the three men stuck to it after they had parted from Smith and the Church of Latter-day Saints he founded, two of them even becoming violent opponents of the new religion. None of the men disavowed his oath.

Two days after revealing the engraved plates to the three men, Smith showed his treasure to eight more witnesses, who were allowed to handle the thin plates and leaf through them. These eight men also testified to the fact with their seals and signatures (2):

Be it known to all nations, kindreds, tongues and people, unto whom this work shall come: That Joseph Smith, Jun., the translator of this work, has shown unto us the plates of which hath been spoken, which have the appearance of gold; and as many of the leaves as the said Smith has translated we did handle with our hands; and we also saw the engravings thereon, all of which have the appearance of ancient work, and of curious workmanship. And this we bear record with words of soberness, that the said Smith has shown unto us, for we have seen and hefted, and know of a surety that the said Smith has got the plates of which we have spoken. And we give our names unto the world, to witness unto the world that which we have seen. And we lie not, God bearing witness of it.

CHRISTIAN WHITMER. JACOB WHITMER. PETER WHITMER JUN. JOHN WHITMER. HIRAM PAGE. JOSEPH SMITH SEN. HYRUM SMITH. SAMUEL H. SMITH.

The oaths of 11 men, not all members of the religious community founded by Joseph Smith, who defended their

Characters which Joseph Smith copied from the metal plates. Scholars classified them as 'reformed Egyptian hieroglyphs'.

ancient faith belligerently and called on their God as witness, carry considerable weight, if we remember the fantastic zeal with which the settlers clung to their congregations and sects for fear of punishment at the Last Judgement.

The two sworn testimonies are not alone in supporting the conclusion that Smith actually possessed the engraved plates for a time, the contents of the translation also support it. They exclude a *complete* forgery, although I am sure there was *partial* forgery.

Smith described the book's golden plates as somewhat thinner than the tin plate commonly used at the time. The individual pages were held together by three rings. The book was some 15 cm broad, 20 cm high and 15 cm thick. A third of the metal pages could be leafed through easily, the other two-thirds being 'sealed' to a block. Smith made copies of the characters on the plates and these were later classified by scholars as 'reformed Egyptian hieroglyphs'.

The present-day Book of Mormon of the Church of Jesus Christ of Latter-day Saints, based on the translations of the mysterious plates by the church's founder Joseph Smith, enlarged by the addition of prophecies about Jesus (which were certainly not in the original text) and a kind of continuation of biblical history, fitted in well with the Christian faith of American society around the middle of the last century.

Smith and his Church of Jesus Christ of Latter-day Saints soon became the object of mockery, but they also attracted the hostility of the American fundamentalists, who stuck rigorously to a literal interpretation of the Bible and preached zealously against critical theology and modern science. There are still fundamentalists in America today.

It was a painful business for Smith because, after their successful translation, the angel Moroni asked for the plates back to hide them again for the distant future. So apart from this translation and the sworn statements of the 11 men, poor Joseph had no proof that he had actually held the legendary plates in his hands every day for nearly two years.

The young Mormon community fought bravely and kept its spirits up. In spite of constant persecution, it increased in size and has 5 million adherents today, although internal strife in the early days led to the arrest of Joseph and his brother Hyrum. On 27 June 1844 a mob broke into the jail at Carthago, Illinois, and shot the brothers Smith. The industrious and God-fearing Mormons had their martyrs. They stuck together and during the last 140 years created a religious and secular empire without parallel.

Between past millennia and the last century there is only a rickety suspension-bridge over a perilous abyss and that is loosely anchored to the banks of time. In spite of that, many rotten planks force researchers to make reckless leaps unless they want to sink in the morass of the present. Two sections of the Book of Mormon, the plates of Ether and Nephi, are well suited to form a fairly solid bridge leading back to past millennia.

The 24 plates of Ether tell the story of the people of Jared. According to the translated plates, the Jaredites are supposed to have pleaded with their God about the time of the building of the Tower of Babel, i.e. towards the end of 3,000 BC, to save them from the warlike turmoil of the neighbouring peoples. God heard their plea and led the Jaredites in a spectacular trek, first into a wilderness and then across the ocean to the coast of America. The journey, described in great detail, lasted 344 days. The plates do not state on which coast of the American continent the emigrants landed, but extracts from the Mormon Bible, Book of Ether, 2. 4 *et seq.*, may be of interest:

And it came to pass that when they came down into the valley of Nimrod [Mesopotamia, E.v.D.] the Lord came down and talked with the brother of Jared; and he was in a cloud and the brother of Jared saw him not.

And it came to pass that the Lord did go before them and did talk with them as he stood in a cloud, and gave directions whither they should travel. And it came to pass that they did travel in the wilderness, and did build barges, in which they did cross many waters, being directed continually by the hand of the Lord.

The barges were small and light upon the water, even like unto the likeness of a fowl upon the water.

And they were built after a manner that they were exceedingly tight, even that they would hold water like unto a dish; and the ends thereof were peaked; and the top thereof was tight and like unto a dish; and the length thereof was the length of a tree; and the door thereof, when it was shut, was tight like unto a dish.

When the Jaredites had built eight windowless watertight vessels according to their 'Lord's' instructions, they thought they noticed a structural error. When the only door was closed, it was pitch black on board, but obviously it was not a mistake, for the 'Lord' gave them 16 gleaming stones, two for each vessel, and the stones gave them bright light for 344 days. Great stuff!

The craft, loaded with seeds and small animals of all kinds, must have been amazingly manoeuvrable in all weathers. Even if the translation of the Book of Ether is only partly factual, the technology the 'Lord' passed on to the Jaredites was sensational. This quotation makes amazing reading:

And it came to pass that they were many times buried in the depths of the sea, because of the mountain waves which broke upon them, and also the great and terrible tempests which were caused by the fierceness of the wind.

And it came to pass that when they were buried in the deep there was no water that could hurt them, their vessel being tight like unto a dish, and also they were tight like unto the ark of Noah; therefore when they were encompassed about by many waters they did cry unto the Lord, and he did bring them forth again upon the top of the waters.

First God created man, then he destroyed his descendants in the Flood. He made a covenant with the survivors 'for all future generations' (Genesis 9.10 *et seq.*). Rebellious mankind tried to rival God and built the mighty tower of Babel. God descended in a rage and scattered the children of men 'over the face of all the earth' (Genesis 11.1 *et seq.*). One of these exiled groups was the Jaredites, who were transported to America in vessels light as birds, with strange sources of light.

If God wanted to give a group of people a chance of survival, what was the point of the laborious construction of eight small vessels? Could not almighty God have carried them to distant parts by a miracle?

Couldn't this God have flown the Jaredites over the ocean or did he prefer not to? Their presence in America shows that he wanted to help them cross the big pond. Was he only able to give technical instructions for ship-building? If he forgot that it was pitch-dark inside the ships, was he forced to correct his error in retrospect by providing flashing stones? Even if the Lord did not want to perform a miracle, even if he made these people work hard for their salvation, why did he not give instructions for building a normal surface craft which could have crossed the Atlantic comfortably? And if the craft had to be like nutshells, almighty God, the acknowledged Lord of the clouds and winds, could at least have given his flock calm seas.

It annoys me that an everlasting omniscient God could not see any farther into the future. Did he not sense that thousands of years after the ocean crossing the traditional account might provoke doubts about his omnipotence? Did it spark the question why technology and not a miracle? He would have been wiser to make use of a miracle which would be inexplicable for all eternity. Miracles escape the bounds of critical reason.

Like all immigrants, the Jaredites sailed to America in terrible conditions. Did not their guardian 'Lord' possess adequate technology to transport his protégés over the big pond in a less dangerous way? What kind of 'God' was at work here 5,000 years ago?

The literature of dark distant ages is literally legendary. We have no precise knowledge. Mankind, stupid and incorrigible, has always managed to wipe out the traditions of previous ages. The library of the ancient city of Pergamon in Asia

Minor, with its 500,000 volumes, was destroyed. The great libraries of ancient Jerusalem and Alexandria were destroyed; the libraries of the Aztecs and Maya went up in flames. Successive generations of mankind wiped out the collected wisdom of the past, but they did not wipe it out completely. There still exist fragments of age-old traditions from which, with a little ingenuity, we can form conceptions of the 'gods' who were once active. We cannot now determine the age of the traditions from textual fragments. The chroniclers noted down indiscriminately not only what they experienced, but also what they knew only from hearsay. Primeval, old and 'new' stories were woven into a colourful tapestry. The chonological course of events was mixed as if in a cocktail-shaker. The years drew rings, but over the centuries collected around a central point.

All we have to do today is to peel off the layers of this 'onion' in order to reveal the essential core. Getting at the 'hard core' is not really miraculous or inexplicable. It is a matter for reason, i.e. analysis, and hence explicable. Working outwards from the centre of tradition — freed of chance superficial accretions — we can find trails which were once expounded for curious men in the distant future. This future has actually begun!

The *Sagen der Juden von der Urzeit* (3) (Legends of the Jews from Primitive Times) relate that, after the banishment from Paradise, the angel Raziel gave Adam a book 'at the behest of the All Highest', the text of which was clearly engraved 'on a sapphire stone'.

Raziel told Adam that he could educate himself with the help of this book. Our first ancestor realised how valuable the 'book' was and after reading it he always hid it in a cave.

Adam learnt from the engravings:

> everything about his limbs and veins and all things that went on inside his body and their purpose and causes. He also learnt about the courses of the planets. With the aid of the book he could ... examine the paths of the moon and the paths of Aldebaran, Orion and Sirius. He could name the names of every separate heaven and knew wherein the activity of each one consisted ... Adam knew all about the rolling thunder, he could tell the action of lightning and could narrate what would happen from moon to moon.

A 'book' on a sapphire stone giving anthropological and astronomical instruction? The heavenly messenger Raziel's gift to Adam is as grotesque as the one Moroni gave to Joseph Smith!

For chroniclers in the remote past all this must have been rather like what journalists today call a canard, a phoney story. This 'book' on a sapphire stone was sheer nonsense.

As clever children of the computer age, we know that things that were once inconceivable are technically possible now. Everyone knows that technology uses tiny silicon chips on which to 'engrave', i.e. store, millions of bits of information. Looking at it from a modern point of view we may ask ourselves if the transmission of a text on a sapphire stone was the product of an advanced technology already far ahead of our own.

The *Sagen der Juden von der Urzeit* has it that Adam handed the book down to his son Seth and that it was inherited by his descendants Enoch, Noah, Abraham, Moses, Aaron and then by Solomon (c. 965–926 BC), the King of Judah and Israel, who acquired his enormous wisdom from the sapphire stone.

According to the *Sagen der Juden von Urzeit*, the Book of the Prophet Enoch was supposed to have formed part of Adam's sapphire book. Enoch, the seventh of the ten patriarchs, was in direct touch with God and spoke to the 'Watchers of the Heavens' and the 'fallen angels'. At the age of 365 he was carried up to heaven — without dying — in a spectacular fashion. Ancient Jewish legends go on to say that Enoch acquired his all-embracing knowledge from Adam's book and that men gathered round him so that he could spread the wisdom of the sapphire stone, teach and instruct them:

When the men sat around Enoch and Enoch spoke to them, they raised their eyes and saw the form of a steed come down from heaven, and the steed descended to earth in a storm. Then the people told Enoch and Enoch spoke unto them: This steed has descended for my sake. The time has come and the day when I go from you and from which day forth I shall never see you again. Then the steed was there and stood before Enoch and all the children of men saw it clearly.

Ancient Jewish tradition describes how the faithful did not

want to let Enoch go after his eloquent farewell before his ascent into heaven, how they ran after him and how he bade them seven times to leave him alone, how he insistently warned them to turn round, for otherwise they would die. It says that small groups of people went home after each warning, although the most persistent stayed with Enoch. Loyalty, devotion, curiosity? In the end Enoch gave up; he lost his temper!

As they insisted on going with him, he spoke to them no longer, and they followed him and did not turn back. And on the seventh day it came to pass that Enoch rode up to heaven in a storm on fiery steeds in fiery chariots.

The ancient Jewish legend shows that events at Enoch's take-off for heaven unfolded in the most 'ungodly' way. When things had quietened down, those who had heeded Enoch's warning and returned home went looking for their friends who had stuck to the prophet until the countdown. They all lay dead around the launching-pad — excuse me — the spot from which Enoch ascended with the fiery steeds.

The legendary age between Adam's appearance in the scenario of the history of mankind and the building of the tower of Babel was the first great age of the gods, of fire-breathing horses, mysterious deaths and remarkable births.

The story, then, is as old as the hills, although we have only known about it since 1947. That was when sensational finds were made in eleven mountain caves at the north-west end of the Dead Sea, near Qumran. They consisted of numerous manuscripts from the second century BC written on leather scrolls concealed in earthenware jars.

One scroll tells the story of Lamech, Noah's father and patron of nomads and musicians.

Even on the Other Side, Lamech will be glad that his intimate family history was not generally known during his lifetime, it was so painful and remarkable. Lamech's wife Bat Enosh gave birth to a child, although the head of the family had never slept with her. Later Lamech learnt from his grandfather Enoch that the 'Watchers of the Heavens' had placed the seeds in Bat Enosh's womb. Lamech showed great generosity and recognised the child as his own. The offspring produced in this remarkable way was called Noah at the request of the 'Watchers'. The same Noah became world famous as a survivor of the Flood.

To make matters worse, the arrival of an unnaturally begotten child in the family of Lamech's son Nir could not be concealed. Nir was married to Sopranima and she was barren, to the family's sorrow. Nir tried hard to implant progeny in Sopranima's womb, but without success. For a priest of the Almighty like Nir, admired by the common people for his wisdom, it was a terrible scandal to learn that Sopranima was barren. Nir was shattered and reviled his wife so grossly that she collapsed and died, although a boy the size of a three-year-old crawled out of his mother's womb. Nir summoned Noah. They buried Sopranima and called the little boy Melchizedek, thenceforth known as the legendary priest-king of Salem, later Jerusalem (5).

Tradition leaves us in no doubt that Melchizedek was a case of a 'divine birth'. Before the Lord opened the sluices to unleash the Flood, the Archangel Michael came down from heaven and informed adoptive father Nir that it was the 'Lord' who had implanted the boy in Sopranima's womb. Consequently, and we can understand this, the Lord had sent him, Archangel Michael, with orders to carry the boy Melchizedek to Paradise so that he would survive the imminent deluge safely:

> And Michael took the boy on the very night on which he had descended and took him on his wings and set him in the Paradise of Eden.

Melchizedek survived! He reappears after the Flood. Moses tells us about it:

> After his return from the defeat of Ched-or-laomer and the kings who were with him, the king of Sodom went out to meet him at the Valley of Shaveh (that is, the Kings' Valley). And Melchizedek king of Salem brought out bread and wine; he was priest of God Most High. And he blessed him and said, 'Blessed be Abram by God Most High, maker of heaven and earth, and blessed be God Most High, who has

delivered your enemies into your hands!' And Abram gave him a tenth of everything.

(Genesis 14.17–20)

Hundreds of Old Testament scholars and exegetists have been excited by this passage from the Bible. 'The strange figure of the priest — king of Salem, who appears like a *deux ex machina* and then vanishes again — has naturally interested posterity' (8).

Obviously, because something extraordinary happened here. Abraham, the first of the three Patriarchs, stands at the head of Jewish tradition. Then the almost unknown Melchizedek comes along and blesses him! And that is not all. Of his own accord, the patriarch gives the king of Salem 'a tenth of everything!' What kind of a priest of 'God Most High' was that? After all, there was only the one God, whom Abraham worshipped. Or did Abraham know anything about the most extraordinary 'divine' birth? Melchizedek appears unexpectedly; he cannot be fitted into any tailor-made accepted pattern.

Given a little less naive faith and a little more courage, the Melchizedek mystery could be solved by modern speculation in this way. An extraterrestrial crew made up of so-called gods produced Noah and Melchizedek by artificial insemination. The legal fathers, Lamech and Noah, recognise them as their own sons, but against their better judgement, for they remember the assurances that the sons of the heavenly ones would be responsible for the artificial insemination of their wives Bat Enosh and Sopranima. It was the same heavenly gods who destroyed their descendants because their genetic experiment did not develop as they liked. Saved from the Flood, both were the products of genetic manipulation. As captain of the ark Noah became founder of the new generation and the priest king Melchizedek became its teacher.

The fact that Melchizedek existed both before and after the Flood does not conflict with this theory. What Albert Einstein calculated with his special theory of relativity and what was proved in physical experiments makes it possible. If Melchizedek, thanks to Archangel Michael's friendly cooperation, boarded a spaceship that accelerated to very high speeds and came straight back to earth, decades or centuries would have passed on earth, whereas the crew of the spaceship would not have aged significantly before they landed again. Melchizedek would still be young and eager for new tasks.*

It is not a question of names or the lapse of time. 'Legendary' traditions cannot be arranged chronologically. Was the survivor of the Flood really called Noah, as the Bible claims? Or was his name Utnapishtim, as it says in the Sumerian *Epic of Gilgamesh*, which dates from c. 2,000 BC? Or was the survivor of the Flood not even called Utnapishtim, but Mulkueikai, as the Kágaba Indians of Colombia name the priest who survived the Flood in a magic craft? Names are unimportant. What matters is the substance of the traditions.

Have we lost sight of Joseph Smith's Book of Mormon? What have the angel Raziel, Enoch's ascent into heaven and the artificial procreation of Noah and Melchizedek got to do with the Book of Mormon?

In the Book of Ether translated by Smith it says that the Jaredites were sent to sea in their eight ships around the time of the building of the Tower of Babel. The Jaredites were led by one of Jared's brothers and Jared himself was Enoch's father!

Jared means something like 'He who has come down', so it is understandable that the Jaredites were a race from a 'divine line' and so enjoyed the privilege of being introduced to a new country by the gods after the Flood. The crew of the spaceship looked after their descendants. They seem to me to have invented the nepotism so widely practised today.

To recapitulate, in the Book of Ether the Jaredites come to their new home in eight windowless ships, each one as tight as a dish. A similar crossing is described in the Babylonian didactic poem about the creation, the *Enuma elis*. It, too, gives an account of the Flood, but this time the survivor is called Atrahasis (9). In the partially preserved epic the god Enki gives the man chosen for survival, Atrahasis, precise instructions for building the ship. In answer to Atrahasis' objection that he knows nothing about ship-building, Enki draws the outline of a ship on the ground and enlightens him.

The American orientalist Zecharia Sitchin, the first scholar bold enough to interpret Sumerian, Assyrian, Babylonian and biblical texts in a modern way, writes (10) that Enki demanded a well-planned ship, hermetically sealed all round and caulked

---

* See my book *According to the Evidence* (1977) for other biblical characters exposed to the effects of time dilation.

with strong pitch. There were to be no deck or openings so that sun could not shine in. It was to be like an *aspu* ship, a *sulili*, (the same word (soleleth) that is used in Hebrew today for a submarine). Enki asked for the ship to be a MA-GUr-Gur (a ship that can roll and be tossed about).

Joseph Smith held the gold plates in his hands in 1827. The poor immigrant from Scotland knew neither Aramaic nor ancient Hebrew and he had never seen Sumerian cuneiform writing. Indeed, in the days of the Mormon prophet there was no scholar in the world who could have deciphered the Babylonian tablets, because, like the Epic of Gilgamesh, they were not discovered until after Joseph Smith's death. So how can we explain the similarities between the Book of Ether and the other texts discovered later?

Our contemporaries see history through glasses polished by scholars. In so far as glasses from the workshops of the exact sciences — mathematics, physics, biology and chemistry, for example, — are concerned, they improve the sight. But since theology and psychology have been given the status of sciences, the glasses have become blurred. Those two disciplines should have been left to the blissful field of faith. When theologians and psychologists agitate old texts in the cocktail-shaker of their specialties, only turbid faith trickles out. And we are supposed to swallow that as if it were a scientific conclusion!

Although expressed more elegantly in the circumlocutions of scientific parlance, it is clearly insinuated that the old chroniclers lied. Driven into a corner, they would be more willing to agree (which archaeologists, ethnologists and pre-historians do not) that men were already capable of building seaworthy ships thousands of years ago than that they involved 'gods', alien teachers, in their logical calculations.

Did the chroniclers of the *Enuma elis* epic lie when they wrote that Atrahasis was instructed in ship-building by the god Enki? Why had Noah and Utnapishtim to be given the idea of building watertight and weatherproof ships by gods? In what magic workshop was the artificial lighting for the Jaredites' fleet cooked up? If there were no savants, how can we understand the 'miracle' of artificial fertilisation that nevertheless brought two splendid types like Noah and Melchizedek into the world?

I know that Noah is not a unique case! The oldest Sumerian

Noah was not even Utnapishtim, but the still older Ziusudra. This example clearly shows that various chroniclers obviously (a) drew on earlier sources and (b) gave former heroes the names of their own people. No matter under what names the conquerors of the Flood appear in the ancient traditions, they were all of semi-divine origin. The protagonists were certainly not purely terrestrial!

Anyone who studies the fragmentarily preserved old texts with clear undimmed glasses finds special characteristics to identify the 'gods' by.

Unlike the God dominating the universe, the divine figures of legend and myth were by no means omnipotent. They did not appear like fairies who moved groups of people from one place to another with a wave of their magic wand. To be sure, the 'gods' themselves flew across countries and even took passengers with them in certain cases, but they did not transport groups of men in their varied types of vehicle. This clearly implies that the 'gods' did not use giant spaceships, their technical capabilities being far too limited. We can assume that their craft were more probably a mixture of shuttle and helicopter. The NASA engineer Josef Blumrich has conclusively proved from the Book of Ezekiel that a mini-spaceship could have been constructed in biblical times (11).

A large mother ship in the earth's orbit that men from the Blue Planet never saw launched smaller craft in the direction of the earth. As in the American space shuttle, there was only room for a small crew. Outside the earth's atmosphere the mini-spaceship fell slowly, braked by its ram jet drive, into the thicker atmospheric layers of the earth. The ram jet drive got its energy from a nuclear reactor. (Opponents of atomic energy will complain that the crew would have been contaminated by radioactivity. Nonsense. Why are sailors not contaminated after long voyages in nuclear-powered submarines?)

The mini-spaceship stopped some 10 km above the earth. Then two or three helicopter units firmly attached to the mini-spaceship emerged. (Helicopters with rotor blades cannot emerge, scoff the sceptics. They can, because they are built to fit inside each other, like a car radio aerial. But what about energy? The main reactor supplied that.) The shuttle glided to earth by means of the helicopters and was in a position to land on plains or mountainous terrain. Fantasy? Where did the

The small spaceship which the NASA engineer Josef F. Blumrich constructed from the details given in the Book of Ezekiel.

extraterrestrials get their knowledge of the atmospheric layers near the globe and the sort of rotor blades suitable for the given conditions? Miles ahead of the inhabitants of the earth, technologically speaking, they had discovered the conditions while in orbit. Besides, a ship's propeller drives a ship in any liquid medium, fresh or salt water, oil or a sea of whisky. Aircraft constructors have long since solved the problem of adjusting rotor blades to the right angle for the prevailing atmospheric pressure.

Incidentally, helicopter landings explain the noise, the thunder and uproar which all the ancient chroniclers describe as accompanying the arrival of the 'gods'.

Obviously large masses of people cannot be transported in small shuttle craft. If a 'god', one of the Most High, wanted to settle a group of peoples on the other side of the ocean, he had to impart instructions about ship-building, as tradition tells us.

Today most ethnologists agree that there were contacts between the Old and the New Worlds, via the Bering Strait or across the Atlantic on simple rafts, as Thor Heyerdahl proved by his own voyages (12). Undoubtedly there were many features common to the civilisations of South and Central America, and those of the Near East, as the following examples show:

Near and Middle East	South and Central America
Accurate calendar calculations among the Sumerians, Babylonians and Egyptians	The same is true of the Inca and (later) the Maya
The ability to cut megalithic stone monsters out of the rock. Practised by the Sumerians, Babylonians, Egyptians and other peoples	Pre-Inca tribes and the Inca possessed the same technical ability. Examples at Tiahuanaco, Bolivia and Sacsayhuaman, Peru
Dolmans and menhirs in Galilee, Samaria, Judea (13) also in prehistoric England and France	Similar examples in Colombia
Mummification	Also found
Prehistoric astronomically	The same finds in

Near and Middle East	*South and Central America*
aligned stone circles and rectangles	prehistoric Peru and Colombia
Enormous markings on the ground that point to the sky in the deserts of present-day Saudi Arabia	The same phenomenon in Peru (Nazca, Palpa) and on the coastal cliffs of Chile
Marriage between brothers and sisters among the Babylonians and Egyptian Pharaohs	Incest also among the Inca to preserve the 'divine blood' of the Sun God
Stories of the Flood, including details such as the dove and the raven which signalled the survivors to leave the ark, among the Sumerians, Babylonian and Egyptians	The same tradition among the Kágaba Indians of Colombia and (later) the Aztecs of Mexico The Aztec Noah was called Tapi The Aztec Flood epic is identical with the biblical one
Skull deformation of small children among the Egyptians	The same deliberate deformation among pre-Inca and Inca tribes
Depictions of cranial surgery on living patients among the Babylonians and Egyptians	The same trepannings among the Inca and Central and North American Indians
Great engineering skill in the building of extensive irrigation systems among the Babylonians	The same skill shown by the Inca and Maya. Recently vast canal systems built by the Maya have been mapped from aircraft and satellites (14)
Feather headdresses or crowns were worn to show that people had an affinity with 'that which flies'. Shown to have been used by Egyptian and Hittite popular leaders	The same custom among the Inca and all Indian tribes
Adoration of the 'flying	Inca and Maya edifices

Near and Middle East

snake' among the
Babylonians, Egyptians,
Hittites and other
Mesopotamian peoples

Building pyramids to
honour the gods and get
closer to them

In Genesis 11.1 it says:
'Now the whole earth had
one language and few
words ...'

In Exodus 14.16 the Lord
says to Moses: 'Lift up
your rod and stretch out
your hand over the sea and
divide it, that the people of
Israel may go on dry
ground through the sea.'

South and Central America

teem with 'flying snakes'

The steeply rising step
pyramids of the Maya do
not resemble the less steep
unstepped pyramids near
Cairo, but there were step
pyramids in Egypt, too,
e.g. at Sakkara. The
massive pyramid of
Teotihuacan, Mexico, is
comparable to the
Egyptian pyramids. The
Mesopotamian ziggurats
are stepped forerunners of
the pyramids

In the Popol Vuh, (15) the
Quiché Maya creation
myth, in the chapter on
'Completion of Creation'
we read: 'they had a single
language. They prayed to
neither wood nor stone ...'
and in the chapter
'Wanderers through the
Night': 'Lost are we.
Whence the confusion? We
had one language when we
came to Tula.'

In the traditions of the
Cakchiqueles, a branch of
the Maya, we read: 'Let us
plunge the tips of our rods
into the sand under the sea
and we shall rapidly
control the sea above the
sand. Our red rods, which
we received before the

Near and Middle East

South and Central America
gates of Tula, will aid us
... When we came to the
edge of the sea, Balam
Quitze touched it with his
rod and straightway a way
was opened.'

Exodus 14.21: 'Then Moses
stretched out his hand over
the sea; and the Lord
drove the sea back by a
strong east wind all night,
and made the sea dry land,
and the waters were
divided. And the people of
Israel went into the midst
of the sea on dry ground,
the waters being a wall to
them on their right hand
and their left.'

Popol Vuh, chapter
entitled 'Wanderers
through the Night': 'They
scarcely noticed how they
crossed the sea. They
crossed it as if there were
no sea. Round stones rose
from the sand and over the
rows of stones did they
walk into it. They called
the place drifting sand;
those who crossed the
parting sea have the name.
Thus did they manage to
cross.'

Genesis 9.12: 'This is the
sign of the covenant which
I make between me and
you and every living
creature that is with
you ...'

Popol Vuh, chapter
'Departure of the
Patriarch': 'This will
succour you when you call
on me. This is the sign of
the covenant. But, now,
heavy of heart, I have to
go.'

Daniel 3.21: 'Then these
men were bound in their
mantles, their tunics, their
hats and other garments
and they were cast into the
burning fiery furnace ...
(25) He answered, "But I
see four men loose,
walking in the midst of the
fire, and they are not hurt;
and the appearance of the

Popol Vuh, chapter 'Ball
Game and Kingdom of the
Dead': 'Then those men
went into the fire, into a
fire house. Within all was
burning heat, but they did
not burn. Smooth of body
and fair of face did they
appear in the twilight.
People wished them dead
in the places where they

Near and Middle East	*South and Central America*
fourth is like a son of the	walked, but it did not
gods."'	happen. Confusion seized
	those of Xibalba.'

It would be useful to expand the small list of the staggering concordances between ancient texts of the Old and New Worlds in a dissertation the size of a large volume, if there were any real interest in explaining unsolved mysteries of the past.

Thor Heyerdahl drew attention to still more parallels, such as identical techniques for weaving cotton, the similarity in the circumcision of boys, the same gold filigree work and so on (12). The scientific journalist Gerd von Hassler confirmed astonishingly similar names given to gods and cities on both continents (16).

The Popol Vuh removes the last doubt about the importation of civilisation into South and Central America from the Mesopotamian region. It states clearly that the Patriarchs came from the East:

> Thus did they vanish and go thither, Balám Quitzé, Balam Acab, Mahucutáh and Jqu Balám, *the first men who came over the sea from the beginning of the sun*. They came hither a long time ago. They died at a great age. And they were called 'Servants of God', Sacrificers' ... *and they brought the writings of Tula over the sea*. They called the scripture that wherein their history was written.

In 1519, when the Spanish conquerors were camped outside Tenochtitlan, Mexico, the Aztec ruler Moctezuma (1466–1520) made an impressive speech to the priests and important dignitaries. It began as follows: 'You know, as I do, *That our forefathers did not come from this country* in which we live, but that they came here *from far, far away* under the guidance of a great prince.'

Moctezuma was a highly cultured ruler of his people, well versed in the sciences of his day, and he had a thorough knowledge of the traditions of his ancestors. He knew what he was talking about. He saw the arrival of the Spaniards under Hernando Cortez as the fulfilment of his belief in the return of the god Quetzalcoatl and so he offered no resistance.

The question no longer arises *whether* civilisations were effectively influenced. What matters is to try to answer the question *when* and *why* they were influenced.

It is pointless to puzzle about the WHEN. In spite of the existence of artefacts which can be dated archaeologically, there is not even an approximate chronology. The Aztecs already referred to ancient traditions, the origins of which they knew nothing. The same was true of the Maya and the Inca. The chroniclers of the day had not experienced what they wrote about: 'It is written in the records of the fathers.' Without quoting sources, I should warn the reader. The authors did not know who these fathers were or when they immigrated.

However, archaeological datings go steadily further back into the past. In *Scientific American*, (18) the celebrated American Maya scholar Norman Hammond mentioned finds of pottery from Yucatán, the northern peninsula between the Gulf of Mexico and the Caribbean, dating to 2,600 years BC. Some of the pre-classical Maya periods may be calculated from the artistic motifs represented on the pottery. The new date confuses us considerably; for according to the previous view held by archaeologists the ancient Maya kingdom was supposed to have begun c. 600 BC and the pre-classical Maya period c. 900 BC at the earliest. So what are we to make of these troublesome potsherds, which are a good 1500 years too old to fit into their theory? Scholars would dearly love to reinter them and forget all about them, leaving a tough nut for future generations to crack. Each new dating complicates the puzzle and yet we anticipate many new finds. The latest academic conclusion is that there is nothing definite about when the legendary immigration took place from either written or archaeological evidence. Dates are still shrouded in the mists of the history of mankind.

HOW the great journey took place is equally obscure. The Bering Strait, icebound in spring and winter, which lies between Cape Prince, Alaska, and Cape Desnef, Siberia, suggests itself as a route. Even today navigation is difficult at all times of the year, owing to drift-ice and fog. This dangerous sea route sounds impracticable for peoples migrating thousands of years ago. But if we postulate rafts, canoes or primitive sailing ships as vehicles for an Atlantic crossing, we must accept that the goal of the journey was known in advance.

I do not underestimate the courage in undertaking bold ventures shown by our ancestors just out of the Stone Age, I even credit them with audacity in times of peril, but not with a penchant for suicide. As land-lubbers they were certainly afraid of the stormy seas which could crush their miserable rafts like nutshells. But if they did risk the perilous expedition, they must have been sure of a worthwhile goal. If we admit that, the question WHY becomes pretty clear. The 'gods' promised them a blessed country far, far away! This promise made it necessary for them to instruct their protégés in the arts of ship-building, navigation, etc. They showed the small groups of people — it was not a mass migration — the route to the goal. Just as it says in the traditions.

There remains the speculation about what reason the 'gods' may have had for the distribution of small groups of people in various parts of the world. Were they concerned with training their semi-divine offspring in new, safe territories? Did they foresee in outline the future evolution of humanity, the direction the further development of their intelligence would take? Lastly, did they expect that among the progeny of the artificially produced Noah and Melchizedek there might be scientists who would find and understand the 'divine' legacy? Were they sure that the trails they laid could never be lost?

Living creatures are subject to certain patterns of behaviour whether they like it or not. At night mosquitoes fly towards the light: they cannot help it. Man must eat and drink in order to live, whether it suits him or not. These are vital functions of the organism.

Intelligent reason asks questions whether it wants to or not. Intelligence wants to know what it was like in the past and how we became what we are. Who originated the idea that *homo sapiens* is different from animals? This series of intelligent questions leads unerringly back to the 'gods', whether we like it or not. Intelligent questioning can only be temporarily interrupted by fake answers; it suddenly finds itself dissatisfied with half-truths. Intelligence is an untameable beast. It keeps on asking what things were like in the past. And in the end it realises that the history of mankind without the 'gods' leads into a landscape, the map of which is blank.

Myth and legend are impregnated with the enormous impression the 'gods' made on primitive man. Chroniclers

Joseph Smith (1805–44), the founder of the Church of Jesus Christ of
Latter-day Saints.

Imaginative painting of the vision of Moroni, the heavenly messenger.

Salt Lake Temple - WOO4335

The Mormon Temple in Salt Lake City.

The village square of Chavín de Huantar.

The road led upwards through a rust-coloured gorge in a series of acute hairpin bends.

picked up the red thread of tradition and spun it further. That is how the 'divine' deeds were recorded, down from their thunderous arrival to the manifold didactic instructions to the inhabitants of the earth. With their abilities our early ancestors transformed what they had learnt into architectonic master-pieces, made use of 'anachronistic' technology and created amazing objects of art.

The Popol Vuh, one of the great books from the dawn of mankind, shows how deliberately the trails were laid. It says that the servants of God 'brought the writings of Tula across the sea. They called the scripture that wherein their history was written.' The ancient traditions of the Quiché Maya refer to yet older writings and part of the Book of Mormon consisted of such writings. Joseph Smith translated the crossing of the Atlantic by the Jaredites from the 24 plates of the Book of Mormon, which form only the smallest part.

Smith translated most of the book from the plate called Nephi. Who was Nephi? He was the son of a Jewish family who lived in Jerusalem around 600 BC, i.e. thousands of years after the Jaredites. His father was called Lehi, his mother Sariah.

In chapter 1, verse 4 of the Book of Mormon, Nephi writes:

For it came to pass in the commencement of the first year of the reign of Zedekiah, king of Judah ... there came many prophets prophesying unto the people that they must repent, or the great city of Jerusalem must be destroyed.

That is right. Jerusalem was completely destroyed in 586 BC. Jeremiah and Ezekiel were prominent in this legendary age. It must have been a special period, for both prophets spoke incessantly with their 'God', who descended from heaven in fire-breathing chariots that made a frightening noise.

Nephi's father Lehi repeated the experiences of the prophets, as is described in Nephi, 1.6 *et seq.*:

And it came to pass as he prayed unto the Lord, there came a pillar of fire and dwelt upon a rock before him ... he saw one [an angel] descending out of the midst of heaven, and he beheld that his lustre was above that of the sun at noon-day.

The being from the pillar of fire ordered Lehi to assemble

Sariah, his sons and daughters (Nephi being among them), and friends of the family in order to inform them that they were destined to travel to a distant country. After initial difficulties, the migrant group built a ship under the guidance of the mysterious Lord: 'And it came to pass that the Lord spake unto me, saying: Thou shalt construct a ship, after the manner *which I shall show thee, that I may carry thy people across the water* (1 Nephi 17.8).

As if that was not enough, the mysterious alien gave the ship-builders special astronauts' food which needed neither preparation nor cooking. He knew that eating keeps body and soul together, but also that another object was even more important — a compass!

> And it came to pass that as my father arose in the morning, and went forth to the tent door, to his great astonishment he beheld upon the ground a round ball of curious workmanship. And within the ball were two spindles; and the one pointed the way whither we should go into the wilderness . . . And we did follow the directions of the ball, which led us in the more fertile parts of the wilderness.

Father Lehi died during the crossing. Nephi assumed command. Nephi's brothers were jealous because of the special favour the 'Lord' showed him and they tied him to a ship's beam. In this tricky situation, they found out how indispensable the compass was. 'And it came to pass that after they had bound me insomuch that I could not move, the compass, which been prepared of the Lord, did cease to work.'

The Mutiny on the Bounty came to an end and the expedition reached the American continent, with the metal plates and the compass: 'Now I, Nephi, had also brought the records which were engraven upon the plates of brass; and also the ball or compass, which was prepared for my father by the hand of the Lord.' (II Nephi 5.12).

Following Nephi's account, Mormon scholars are convinced that the group first wandered from the Red Sea through the Arabian peninsula, then built their ship on the coast of the Indian Ocean, somewhere in the area of the Gulf of Aden and Oman, and finally reached the coast of South America across the South Pacific. James E. Talmage (19) puts this around 590 BC, a date we should take note of.

There is one amazing coincidence. The translation that Joseph Smith made from the metal plates in 1827 is duplicated in the Popol Vuh. But Smith could not possibly have known the contents of the Quiché Maya bible, for it was only translated for the first time by Wolfgang Gordan in the 1950s!

Two groups reached the American continent independently of each other. First, the Jaredites in their hermetically sealed ships in the age of the first wave of the gods. It was the legendary epoch in which flourished the chroniclers of Adam's sapphire book, Enoch's ascent into heaven, the test-tube babies Noah and Melchizedek, as well as the 'lords' of creation Utnapishtim, Ziusudra and others. Secondly, the Nephites, who set out from the east and reached South America thousands of years later, around 590 BC.

Soon after the landing Nephi had a temple built:

And I, Nephi, did build a temple; and I did construct it after the manner of the temple of Solomon save it were not built of so many precious things. But the manner of the construction was like unto the temple of Solomon; and the workmanship thereof was exceeding fine.

(II Nephi 5.16)

It is not my concern to prove which parts of the Book of Mormon are genuine, but it may please the followers of the Church of Jesus Christ of Latter-day Saints that one proof emerges as a by-product of my researches.

Nephi built a temple 'after the manner of the temple of Solomon'. In so far as this information is valid, South America must contain a temple (on a smaller scale) of the kind Solomon had built in Jerusalem — a complex with outer and inner courts, a sanctuary with a temple which had four doors aligned on the four cardinal points of the compass. This temple must have originated between the fifth and sixth centuries BC.

Moreover, Nephi's temple must have been built 'cold', so to speak, without prototypes or borrowings from typical South American architecture. The temple must have been the first of its kind, an edifice that appeared out of the blue without local traditions.

I am not only on the trail of a temple which meets these pre-requisites, I am also on the trail of the 'Lord' who led the Nephites to South America. Did this 'god' still exist after the landing or had he transformed himself into spirit? Also, where did Nephi recruit the large numbers of builders needed? After all, he arrived with only a small group. 'Immediately after their arrival, the Nephites began ... to till the earth, and we began to plant seeds: yea, we did plant all the seeds which we had brought from the land of Jerusalem' (I Nephi 18.24).

The Nephites produced progeny assiduously, for they practised polygamy (forbidden to the Mormons by government decree in 1890). Assuming that the immigrant group consisted of 100 men and 100 women, and each woman bore one child a year, the Nephites would have numbered 1,500 souls in 15 years. The firstborn, pubescent teenagers of 15 followed the example of their elders and willingly played their part in multiplying. In 30 years a good 5,000 Nephites would praise their 'Lord'. Quite enough people to build the temple, especially as there were indigenous workers to collaborate with them. The personnel was there.

The Lord was present! As soon as he arrived, he gave Nephi this task: 'And it came to pass that the Lord commanded me, wherefore I did make plates of ore that I might engraven upon them the record of my people' (I Nephi 19.1).

Thirty years later. The 'Lord' set great store by a complete log book. Once again he ordered Nephi:

And thirty years had passed away from the time we left Jerusalem. And it came to pass that the Lord God said unto me: Make other plates; and thou shalt engraven many things upon them which are good in my sight, for the profit of thy people.

Was the 'Lord' vain? Why did he want the 'Things ... which are good in my sight' noted down? The 'Lord' constantly insisted upon his golden words being engraved upon the metal plates. He considered them important for the future, otherwise he would have had them recorded on perishable materials such as papyrus, leather or wood. This 'Lord' in his wisdom took care that his communications, addressed to intelligent beings in the future, were permanent.

A difficult question. Is there a temple in South America modelled on Solomon's masterpiece? Is there some proof of the activities of the gods to be found there?

I invite you to visit that temple.

2 *In the Beginning Everything Was Different*

Drawing the attention of the masses to something means putting
healthy human reason on the right track.'
Gotthold Ephraim Lessing (1729–81)

The Jerusalem of the Andes is called Chavín de Huantar.

It was raining cats and dogs on that April day in 1980 when
two young missionaries, soaked to the skin, stood outside the
door of our house in Feldbrunnen. The older one, about 30
years old, was an American called Charlie, the younger man's
name was Paul and he came from Berne. My visitors from the
Church of Jesus Christ of Latter-day Saints made me a present
of the German version of the Book of Mormon. (I already had
seven other translations in my library.) I invited the missionaries to come inside to warm up and drink a cup of coffee.

My fellow countryman Paul asked what I thought of the
Book of Mormon. I said that I found the plates Ether and
Nephi exciting and informative. Nor did I think they were
forgeries, but found it unfortunate that some rather crude
prophecies about Jesus had been added to the original text.

Naturally, the young missionaries disagreed with me. Either
the complete Book of Mormon was inspired by the Holy Ghost
and therefore 'genuine', or the whole book was worthless.
Being well up in the subject, I showed my disinclination for a
discussion that would lead nowhere, a hint that was very
quickly taken by Paul, belying the reputation the Bernese have
for being slow-witted. He asked, 'You know many ruins in
South America. Have you found any that resemble Solomon's
temple in Jerusalem?'

I told him truthfully that I had not. The missionaries said
goodbye without trying to make a hopeless conversion. It was
such a terrible April day that they would certainly have found
a willing victim if they could have promised me blue skies.

Paul, the Bernese, had put a bee in my bonnet which went on
buzzing, but another one was tormenting me even more.

Whether the temple mentioned in the Book of Nephi existed in South America or not seemed far less important to me than the question whether the temple described in detail by the prophet Ezekiel in the Old Testament existed — a temple in a distant land, standing on a high mountain, built like the temple of Solomon. If there were a temple in South America that fitted Ezekiel's description, that *would be* a thrilling story.

What has the Nephi of the Book of Mormon to do with the Ezekiel of the Bible? Well, both of them lived at the same time in the same geographical zone. Perhaps they knew each other. Both of them wrote about a flying god who came down and gave instructions. On this god's orders, Nephi had a temple built in South America and Ezekiel was flown by the same god to a distant land where he was shown a temple on the Solomonic model on a 'very high mountain'.

It is established that Ezekiel lived in Jerusalem and Babylon. If someone showed him the temple in South America — he describes it incredibly accurately — someone must have flown him there and then back to the Near East. There is no other possibility.

So my search for a Solomonic temple in South America was by no means purely inspired by the Book of Mormon, I was also looking for Ezekiel's temple and the trail of the 'flying god', who was at the back of it all. I only realised much later that both trails would meet in the most fascinating way.

My eyes were aching from looking at an endless procession of temples in books on archaeology. At the time finding *the* temple meant more to me than the sight of a blue Mauritius means to a philatelist. If I suspected similarities, the plan of Solomon's temple in Jerusalem told me that essential details were missing, that it was too early or too old, or that it did not belong to the period of Nephi or Ezekiel. I went through 39 lavishly illustrated books. In all of them Chavín de Huantar was described. I decided to visit this site, take accurate measurements and see the landscape in which it lies with my own eyes.

Nineteen eighty-one. Once again Europe was enjoying a cold wet spring. It was autumn in Peru when I rented a kind of Russian jeep, a Lada Niva, in Lima, the capital.

Long before dawn, I was driving along a smooth asphalt road, the Panamericana del Norte, one of the best roads in the world, through sandy desert bordering the coast in the direction of Trujillo, the fourth largest city in Peru. I left the Panamericana at the town of Pativilca. After that sugar-cane plantations lined the road.

When I was handing over 200 soles at a toll station, a horrible stench from the Lada Niva assailed my nostrils. The cap of the petrol tank was missing. I wrapped a piece of plastic round a stone and blocked the stinking hole with it.

After running for 30 km through a stony desert, past the menacing spurs of the mountains, the road began to climb gradually. After turning off from Pativilca — in the distance you can see the ruins of a fortress from the time of the Chimu Indians — I reached the God-forsaken village of Chasquitambo at a height of 780 m. In ancient times this place was a handing-over point for Inca relay runners. Nowadays, too, the best thing is to keep on running.

The ascent into a rust-coloured gorge began in a series of acute hairpin bends. The lowering rain clouds now lay behind me, the fog banks cleared and opened up a panorama of light brown and black mountains.

My clattering Russian banger was becoming less willing with every curve. On the narrow road, my red star could no longer make it in second gear. Near Cajacay, at a height of 2,600 m, the old fellow was completely out of breath. Automobile asthma. The engine needed more oxygen. I unscrewed the top of the air filter. The filter which was supposed to let the air through felt like the remains of a plaster cast. I threw it away, screwed the top on to the empty filter, started and the old jalopy leapt forward. It had understood me. It *had* to get me up the mountain.

After every hairpin bend I hoped I had reached the top of the pass. For a long time these were vain hopes, for more and more mountain valleys kept appearing. The clay huts by the roadside became fewer. Indians in colourful ponchos, carrying heavy bundles on their backs, put one foot before the other in the steady rhythm of the experienced mountain climber. I was amazed that the hard-working local inhabitants could scratch a living from the sterile rocky soil up here, yet a third of Peru's 14.6 million inhabitants live in these uplands.

I reached the cloud-filled pass at a height of 4,100 m. In European latitudes it would have been a zone of permanent ice and snow, but Peru is closer to the Equator. Only dry grasses and miserable stunted bushes grow up here.

A young dark-brown Indian woman, with a baby on her breast in a cloth bag and a heavy sack of potatoes on her back, looked at me suspiciously when I asked her if she would like a lift, because friendly foreigners are rare in this region. I took the sack off her back and pushed it behind the seats of the Lada Niva. She got in and laughed self-consciously after arranging the six skirts that all Indian women wear. We drove past the frozen lagoon of Conocochca with the glaciers of the 6,600 m high Cordillera de Huyauhuish ahead of us.

I managed to worm out of the taciturn Indian woman where she was going — the town of Catac at a height of 3,540 m in the valley of the Rio Santa. I shuddered at the idea of the woman having to walk the 40 km stretch with her heavy burdens — it would have taken her two days, but we did it in half an hour. In Catac the road forks off to Chavín de Huantar.

At the only petrol station I filled my jeep with a young woman and two men. She was called Ruth; Uri and Isaac had black and red beards respectively. They were Israelis who had decided to roam through the world for a year with no fixed plans, although they did not exclude visits to archaeological sites like Chavín de Huantar. They asked why I was going there. I limited myself to vague remarks about a Solomonic temple connected with the prophet Ezekiel. They might be the sort of fanatically orthodox Israelis who would have been shocked by the real object of my research.

'Are you Swiss?' asked Uri. 'Then you must know Erich von Däniken's books. I am not sure whether the ideas he puts forward are crazy or rational.'

Instead of answering I bit my lip.

Beyond Catac the road was not asphalted and led in tortuous curves to the picturesque icy lake of Quericocha at a height of 3,980 m. The snowclad summit of Yanamarey (5,260 m) caught the eye.

Next came the tunnel through the Kahuish pass (4,510 m). The word 'tunnel' might call up false associations with the tunnels in Western industrial countries but I should point out that this 500 m long specimen is only hacked roughly out of the rock with an unmade road, full of potholes, running through it. Icy water drips from roof and walls and there are no lights or signals in the one track nightmare road. If the head-lights of an oncoming car appear, the driver nearest the exit or entrance has to back out. Naturally, everyone drives in the hope of not meeting an oncoming car in the dark hole. This tunnel does not deserve a star in the guide books.

If the uphill drive had been taxing, the steep descent on the other side of the tunnel into the Mosna valley proved really frightening, even for a veteran driver like me. The narrow un-made road winds like an endless snake clinging to the mountain in curve after curve. Your eyes cling to the left because a sheer abyss threatens on the right. We reached the bottom of the valley at the little village of Machac (3,180 m). The ruins of Chavín de Huantar are clearly visible, close to the road.

The Hotel Turistas was full to the last bed, not of tourists but archaeologists. We met the crème de la crème of German and Peruvian archaeologists. In the distinguished German group, Professors Udo Oberem and Henning Bischof greeted me politely, and their Peruvian colleagues were polite and friendly. To the Germans I am an unpredictable outsider, always planning some new trick. The Peruvians have a different opinion of me. When I was honoured by the aldermen of the town of Nazca some years ago, the mayor said in his address that there were many theories about the lines on the plain of Nazca. He could not say whether they were a calendar or a take-off point for hot-air balloons, the remains of Inca roads, magical signs, the marking lines of a sportsground or landmarks for extraterrestrials. 'As for those of who live and work here,' said the mayor, 'we are not primarily interested which of the experts is right. But one thing is certain: Herr von Däniken has brought the most tourists to our region!'

Over the evening meal the Israelis asked if they could help me in any way, for they had found out who had given them a lift. I accepted their offer gratefully, for a continuity girl was just what I needed when taking my measurements.

In the morning the Israelis were waiting for me on a sunny hill outside the site of the ruins. They were suitably draped in cameras and measuring apparatus. We passed through the massive wooden gate into the ruins of Chavín de Huantar.

The section of the complex that is still preserved is called El Castillo, the castle, although it never was a castle. It is a rectangular building 72.90 m long and 70 m wide. Large granite blocks, fitting together to the millimetre, form the rectangular façades. The lower monoliths nearest to the ground are the best preserved. The higher the building, which slopes slightly inwards, rises, the more clearly visible are the ravages of time — just like the Solomonic temple in Jerusalem which suffered 36 wars and was destroyed 17 times. At Chavín as in Jerusalem new walls were built each time on the lower blocks of stone.

The main portal of the Castillo faces east, the direction of the sunrise (and Jerusalem). Two columns, topped by a mono-lith nine metres long, are flanked by square and rectangular granite slabs. The squat columns are decorated with incomprehensible patterns in relief, as are the crowning monolith and the adjacent slabs. Weathering through the ages has worn down the reliefs and unfortunately man, too, has damaged the delicate work. When El Castillo first stood there in all its glory, the massive structure must have looked like a single, almost seamless block, even from a short distance. El Castillo was the termination and crown of the temple complex, the Holy of Holies, to which only the high priests had access.

Today a rubbish heap overgrown with clumps of grass is concealed behind the main portal. A few steps lower down lies a square which occupies the whole width of the Castillo — the forecourt of the sanctuary. Some 36 m from the Castillo, more steps lead down to a second gigantic courtyard (70 by 42 m), from which yet more steps lead to the so-called 'sunken square' (the length of the sides are 49.70 m).

To the north and south of the sunken square rise platforms, which have not yet been excavated, but you can recognise the artificial hill by the scattered monoliths protruding from it. The whole site is reckoned to cover an area of some 13 hectares, but so far only the temple complex has been excavated. It is known that the whole layout stood on a man-made stone platform.

Four flights of steps lead from the sunken square to the four cardinal points of the compass with absolute accuracy, as I checked with my own compass. The side of the plateau descends 80 m to the bed of the River Mosna which flows past the temple in a south-easterly direction.

The complex measures 228 m from the western wall of the Castillo to the south-east corner. The section excavated to date is about 175 m wide. These measurements do not include the wall that once enclosed the area. Remains of this wall are visible on the west side.

At all events, a huge rectangular complex stood here with outer and inner courtyards and the (still extant) ten-metre-high Holy of Holies, with inner and outer courtyards for the priests and the people. The rectangle is aligned on the four cardinal points of the compass with its steps and doors and the main portal points to the east, exactly like the Solomonic temple in Jerusalem.

Today Solomon's temple in Jerusalem no longer forms an exact rectangle; it is now an irregular trapezoid, with sides of 315 m to the north, 280 m to the south, 485 m to the west and 470 m to the east (1). However, the original temple was strictly rectangular. King Herod was responsible for the distorted shape, which doubled the area, and because the space was lacking, additional supporting walls were built on which (in those days) new platforms were placed.

Ruth, Uri and Isaac were busy measuring the courtyards, walls and monoliths, while I was taking photographs from every angle and in every corner. When we stopped for a cigarette and Ruth showed me my notepad clipped to a board, I held my breath. This was professional work! With delicate lines she had drawn a site plan that was ready for the printers. All the walls and monoliths, the steps and flights of stairs and the sunken square were sketched in. The beginning and end of the lines were marked by small arrows to show which sections the measurements referred to.

We sat on boulders, which were not in short supply. I asked my new friends what their jobs were. Ruth said drily, 'I am a surveyor for road building and land measurement.'

So that accounted for the professionalism! Uri turned out to be a teacher, Isaac a pilot. The gods had put the right team into my Lada Niva! The four of us did a job which would have taken me four times as long by myself.

Together we explored the network of passages and galleries under Chavín de Huantar. One passage on the east side of the main square was only 1.10 m high and 67 cm wide and it was impossible to stand upright in it. For one very good reason.

On 17 January 1945 Chavín de Huantar was swamped by

a massive flood. It happened like this. The little river Mosna runs past the south-east side; on the north-west side, between the ruins and the Indian village of Chavin, a stream called Huacheqsa tumbles down into the depths. It rises from a mountain lake which is fed by the water melting from a glacier in the cordillera. In December 1944 and January 1945 more water flowed in than the lake could take and the rocky banks broke like a dam. The stream became a raging torrent and covered the low-lying parts of Chavín de Huantar with a dark brown layer of mud which penetrated the underground passages. When the waters subsided, scree, sand and mud were left behind.

The passage through which I crawled with the help of a flashlight was once higher, or deeper, whichever you prefer. When I had gone as far as I could in the passage beneath the ruins, I saw five lateral tunnels, 60 cm high and 48 cm wide. They may have formed part of an irrigation system, especially as the main passage ran in the direction of the river Mosna.

However, as a 1.72 cm high passage on the west side ran in a southerly direction, i.e. not in the direction of a stream, the subterranean infrastructure cannot have been intended to act solely as water mains.

Chavín de Huantar had been flooded in earlier times. In 1919 the Peruvian archaeologist Julio C. Tello carried out extensive excavations with a group of Indians. When he returned in 1934, the stream had 'destroyed part of the main wing' (2). Tello writes that a third of the complex which he had seen when it was still intact was then destroyed and that many subterranean passages and channels had been flushed out. Kilometres away Tello found stone, metal, and pottery artefacts on a sandbank in the river miles from the temple. They had been swept out of the temple ruins.

When the temple first stood there in all its glory, the raging mountain torrents could not have affected it. The closely fitting megalithic walls were watertight, the irrigation channels around and under Chavín de Huantar functioned and the streams were under control. It was only when fallen trees and monoliths hindered the flow of the water and after grave robbers cut holes in the walls of the Castillo that the water could exercise its destructive power on the buildings.

Together we set out to explore the passages which run under Chavín de Huantar in a tortuous network.

The next day my Israelis took a local bus in which the passengers were packed like sardines. I promised I would send them all a copy of my book in Hebrew, with a personal dedication. We had only spent two days together, yet I missed Ruth and the bearded men when I drove my Lada Niva back to the ruins to take a closer look at the passages in the rubbish dump.

Two tunnels on the north side of the Castillo are shut off by iron grilles to stop tourists going into the dark labyrinth on their own. And it is a labyrinth, as I found out.

Just beyond the entrance the first tunnel leads to a remarkable stele, *El Lanzon*, the lance or spear. *El Lanzon* is situated at the intersection of the two passages which are over three metres high, but only 50 cm wide. Monolithic granite slabs form the ceiling.

In spite of its strange proportions, this passage would be hardly worth mentioning if it did not contain an inexplicable puzzle. *El Lanzon* is a giant stele more than four metres high, yet the passages are little more than three metres high. How did *El Lanzon* get here? It is not a rubber giant that could have been bent. Given its great length, it could not have been manoeuvred horizontally around the countless bends in the 50 cm wide passage. There is only one solution. Right from the start, the architects of Chavín de Huantar planned an opening in the ceiling through which the stele could be lowered into the crossing between the two passages, before the rest of the vast temple complex was erected over it.

No one knows how to interpret *El Lanzon*. The Czecho-slovakian archaeologist and ethnologist Miloslav Stingl (3) describes the stele as:

A very strange creature. Large jaguar teeth stick out over the lower lip. The eyes are staring upwards as if they were looking up to heaven. The belt round the god's body is also decorated with jaguar heads. Two snake heads hang from the belt. The god holds his right hand up, the other rests on his hip.

That is a description, not an interpretation, and I find it hard even to follow the description because I cannot recognise a 'creature' in *El Lanzon* at all. True, you can make out a

The stele El Lanzon is situated deep underground at the crossing of the two passages. It is more than three metres high, but only 50 cm wide.

El Lanzon is lavishly adorned with ornaments. No one knows what they mean. There are many explanations, but none which makes sense.

big muzzle with protruding 'jaguar teeth', but not in the place where jaguars normally have their fatal fangs. Where Miloslav Stingl sees jaguar teeth, I recognise — equally imaginatively — joints of armour, since *El Lanzon* strikes me as a technical artefact rather than an animal figure.

Apart from the passage through which I came to confront *El Lanzon*, all the passages leading from the intersection come to a dead end. After a few paces I was halted by massive walls. That struck me as odd. What was the sense of the planners of Chavín de Huantar only completing the passage to *El Lanzon*, and ending all the other tunnels in a mysterious full stop? All that work for an architectural joke? I suspected secret doors behind the dead ends of the passages. No more and no less.

As I could go no farther, I retraced my steps. Outside the sun was blinding as it can only be in the clear air at a height

A menacing helmeted figure blocked my way.

of 3,000 m. I blinked hard and entered the second tunnel which runs southwards under the Castillo. It was lit by weak bulbs along the walls and they suddenly failed. I groped my way back into the daylight. A friendly attendant lent me an old-fashioned carbide lamp. (I gave him my lighter as surety and I was soon to miss it.) The smell reminded me for a moment of my first bicycle.

The harsh light shone on passages three metres high and cut out of the rock, and on the monoliths forming the ceiling. Soon the tunnel branched off to the left and right; I chose the left-hand one.

I nearly fell over a stone head which, at first glance, looked like a helmeted being, possibly humanoid. In the past the walls were covered with reliefs depicting winged figures flying upwards. Today only vestiges remain as evidence. The figures are carved with such delicacy and in such low relief that they might have been made by a modern dentist using a high-speed drill to practise his hobby of sculpting. But nowadays dentists have no time for badly paid hobbies, they prefer to invest in lucrative high-rise buildings. This passage also came to a dead-end formed by a massive wall.

With all the zeal and patience of a Boy Scout, I went back to the main passage, tried a different entrance, climbed seven steep steps and reached another corridor. It was 1.30 m wide and 1.83 m high. Two people could comfortably walk side by side in it. Across the top of the steps ran a narrower passage with three exits leading to three chambers 5.70 m long, 1.94 m wide and 2.25 m high. The harsh light of the carbide lamp revealed grotesque figures. Strange stone heads revealed their helmets and gave me haughty, rather mocking looks. They were asking, 'What do you think of us?'

Many times I tried to find a way through the walls, but could not manage it. I trotted back to the central corridor, made two 90-degree turns on my own axis and entered another room. In it stone heads were neatly arranged on a wooden plank facing reliefs showing all kinds of fabulous scenes. How many more passages and chambers await excavation? Perhaps the secret of the 'gods' awaits discovery deep below the ruins, perhaps the architects preserved the key to the misinterpreted culture of Chavín de Huantar deep underground?

While I scrutinised every square inch of the wall which closed

There are also easily accessible passages — a good 1.80 metres high and 1.30 metres wide.

Deep in the earth stone heads with strange faces stared at me in the harsh light of the carbide lamp.

off the tunnel to see if there was any trace of an opening, the carbide lamp gave up the ghost. I was in darkness. It was as quiet as the grave. For the first time I felt a draught of cold air passing through the chambers. Although I could not see, I felt my way to the source of the draught, stumbling over stone heads and bumping into monoliths. I took several flash-light photos, as I had plenty of batteries. The current of air came from under the floor of the rear wall. Was there a passage behind it leading even deeper into the earth? I fingered the masonry, pulling hard on protruding parts of the blocks, but nothing budged.

I cautiously put one foot ahead of the other, taking flash photos. I sadly missed the lighter I had left with the attendant.

I crawled upwards on all fours.

One passage wall felt much like another; none of them gave a clue where to go. I had to find the stairway whose seven steps I had climbed up and now must climb down again. But the stairway I felt led upwards. The current of air grew stronger along the walls. I crawled upwards on all fours. Another seven steps and I saw light right above me. The tunnel led beneath an iron grille which could easily be lifted up. I hauled myself out of the depths into the open air and tried to decide where I was.

I had come out of the labyrinth roughly in the centre of the Castillo, high above the east-facing main entrance. The huge rectangle of the temple complex spread out below me. I clambered down and sat down under the main gate to catch my breath. I looked up to try to find out which hole I had crawled out of ... and discovered strange flying creatures engraved on the underside of the monolith lying across the columns.

They consisted of 14 cherubs, as the Bible calls the watchers of the heavens. Seven figures resembling birds of prey were looking northwards and seven southwards. It struck me that all the stairways I had ascended or descended had seven steps. Was the 'sacred number seven' the number giving the key to Chavín de Huantar?

The number seven has traditions which are not confined to the seven-year itch. Its magic is invoked in the seven-day periods into which the month is divided. Around 1,600 BC the Babylonians did away with their five-day week and introduced the seven-day week. In the seven celestial bodies, Sun, Moon, Mercury, Venus, Mars, Jupiter and Saturn, the Babylonians saw the whole order of the cosmos. Among the Jews, the seven days of creation and the seven-branched menorah of the tabernacle testify to the importance of the sacred seven. In the Revelation of St John we find the 'book with seven seals'. Seven has significance in Buddhism and Malayan civilisation. In ancient Greece seven days of grace were common. Thebes had its famous seven gates, there were seven wise men ... and then there were the seven wonders of the world. Was the number seven revered in Chavín de Huantar, too?

No code is safe to our modern intelligence services. Surely it should be possible to crack codes that are simply begging for decipherment?

Down below one 'sunken square' a collaborator of the archaeologist Julio C. Tello found an obelisk that today stands in the Archaeological Museum of Lima. It is called the Tello obelisk and its sign language awaits interpretation. I spent hours in front of it, taking photographs and copying the engravings on it. I asked Peruvian archaeologists about the possible meaning of the patterns. I soon realised that they knew nothing definite when they struck up the cult aria: the jaguar cult, the bird of prey cult, etc. I could equally well sing the pyramid cult, as small pyramids can also be made out on the Tello obelisk. Down below the square where the obelisk was found stands the 'Altar of the Seven Goats' (also known as the 'Altar of the Constellation Orion'). My zoological imagination was not powerful enough to make out seven goats, but the arrangement of seven holes in the altar does correspond approximately to the position of the seven satellites in the constellation of Orion.

The Tello obelisk.

Today the Tello obelisk from Chavin de Huantar is housed in the Archaeological Museum at Lima. The engraved ornamentation with its bewildering interplay of images has not yet been 'deciphered'.

The Raimondi stele.

The wretched figure seven crops up everywhere. Specialist literature (4, 5) confirms that it was also a sacred number in Chavín de Huantar. Is seven a key to the messages hidden there? Where is the master spy 007? Perhaps archaeologists should rope in a code-breaker. The old 'cult' caper is pretty hackneyed.

Every visitor to the Museo Antropológico y Arqueológico in the Plaza Bolivar in Lima walks past the Raimondi stele. It comes from Chavín de Huantar. Antonio Raimondi had the stele, made of diorite and measuring 1.75 m high, 73 cm wide, and 17 cm thick, brought to the capital in the year 1873. What do scholars make of the reliefs on this work of art? Let them say their piece.

Miloslav Stingl:

The Raimondi stele ... represents the jaguar man. More and more highly stylised jaguar heads grow from his own divine head with great fangs protruding from their jaws. (3)

Professor H. D. Disselhoff:

A jaguar man stands upright on a rectangular slab. In each hand he holds a composite sceptre, richly ornamented with curves. The lower half ends in the stylised heads of birds of prey, the upper half in a vegetable emblem. The piled-up headdress is composed of the jaws of beasts of prey and snakes' heads ... and snakes' bodies with realistically depicted heads. The main subjects are hybrids made of men and animal, feline beasts of prey, snakes and birds of prey. (6)

Rudolf Pörtner and Nigel Davies:

Represents a figure, front face, with the head of a beast of prey. Both hands hold a decorated staff which reaches far above the figure's head. The upper two-thirds of the stone is filled by an imaginative headdress consisting of suggestions of mouths with tongues hanging out arranged one above the other. From them parallel snakes' heads emerge upwards to left and right. (7)

Professor Hermann Trimborn:

A stone slab, the so-called Raimondi stele, came from here as early as 1873. In low relief it depicts a feline monster with a sceptre in its claws. It is crowned with a series of open jaws belonging to beasts of prey, from which snakes emerge.' (8)

Professor Horst Nachtigall:

This stele is one of the most interesting sculptures of the American megalithic civilisation. It represents an upright half-human half-animal figure with an animal head and a headdress consisting of monsters' heads, framed by a crown of rays. Both hands and feet have animal claws. A snake girdle encircles the body. (5)

Dr Siegfried Huber:

The details of the relief drawings are like codes. Fangs, snakes' heads, mysterious interlacings and eyes with no symbolic explanation — surreal if one can call them anything. The petrified threatening expression of an anxiety-ridden existence. (9)

Dr Friedrich Katz:

Here, too, we find hair snakes and facial features strongly resembling jaguars. The Raimondi stele consists of the stratification of several bodies and faces in an almost monstrous way. (10)

Dr H. G. Franz:

The standing figure represents the religious leader, priest, shaman, call him what you will, in a mask, which appears in a fantastic transformation as a face mask or full head mask with an animal skin. The mask-cum-helmet becomes

a mask-cum-tower ... The feet end in jaguar or eagle claws. The built-up mask rises far above the small stunted figure ... What appears above must be included in the mask's superstructure, which consists of several superimposed animal jaws — wide open dragonlike upper jaws, which at the same time seem tipped upwards. (11)

Dr Inge von Wedemeyer:

The consummate image of the highest incarnation of the god of creation Viracocha. (12)

Gentle reader, you can just as well turn the photographs of the Raimondi stele upside down so that the enigmatic and variously interpreted figure falls from above. Of course the animal claws, the eagle's claws, the feet of the jaguar man or whatever they are supposed to be, would be at the wrong end, but it takes less imagination to recognise that the figure is falling, than to puzzle out all the zoological discoveries which make no sense in the end.

If such contradictory interpretations of the relief code, the only word that seems suitable, can be given, there should also be room for my speculative questions. Surely the peculiar sceptre has a very technical look? Is it a question not of jaguars or stunted jaguar men, with highly stylised heads or towering masks, but of the diagram of a car engine with fuel injectors and many feed pipes? Is it a picture puzzle of some future technology that we shall only understand when we ourselves have developed enough?

I do not know what the stele means, either, but one thing is obvious to me, the archaeological tap dance on the spot will never get us anywhere. People are not brave enough for unorthodox thinking. Arthur Schopenhauer (1788–1860) said that to ignore stems from ignorance. I have nothing more to add.

Chavín de Huantar plays a dirty trick on academics by the mere factor of its existence. The temple complex has no model and so cannot be fitted into a chronological development. Chavín de Huantar emerges suddenly, without any advance warning, saying here I am, the Chavín de Huantar culture. This sudden appearance brings out the sweat of doubt on academic foreheads and confuses the well-trained grey cells.

Quotations from three celebrated scholars echo this confusion.

1. Professor Walter Krickeberg:

It has often been emphasised that the development of higher civilisation in ancient America did not take place as an organic growing process in slow continuous advances, but by leaps and bounds, one might almost say explosively ... the oldest American high civilisations appear on the scene suddenly, apparently without roots or preliminary stages, for example the Olmec culture in Mesoamerica and the Chavín culture in the Andes. This remarkable phenomenon can probably only be satisfactorily explained if we postulate one or more external impulses which affected ancient America. (13)

2. Miloslav Stingl:

The appearance of the Chavín culture is more like an explosion, an unexpected discharge, the effects and consequences of which were felt throughout Peru. (3)

3. Professor H. D. Disselhoff:

I am convinced that *an as yet unexplained external influence* prevailed when the Chavín culture originated. (6)

Chavín de Huantar astonishes everyone who visits it. At the site nearly 50,000 sq. m of uneven rocky terrain were levelled. The first plans for the surface buildings already included an irrigation system deep below them, connecting or emerging corridors were cut (exploded?) out of the rock and the Castillo with all its subsidiary buildings and square matches the subterranean infrastructure exactly. A work of genius, an achievement unique in the world, in so far as it has no prototype. But: the Solomonic temple in Jerusalem also had underground corridors. Recently, more intensive excavations in Jerusalem revealed the hidden passages, and there are still many similarities between the temple layout at Jerusalem and that at Chavín de Huantar awaiting discovery. Archaeological excavations are in progress.

Chavín de Huantar could not have been built without technical know-how. As all scholars agree that such know-how did not exist on the American continent, it must necessarily have been imported. First-class stonemasons were at work, not hastily trained Indians. There were tools which had been developed down the generations by practical use. There were architects experienced in building above and below ground, who planned as a team. When the bare stonework was finished, artists with special skills were waiting to decorate the hundreds of stone slabs with their abstract art. Did they create the style of Chavín de Huantar out of the blue?

In the opinion of all the academics, this style, too, has no models. Was it just there, in all its perfection? Although uninterpreted as yet, the drawings of the flat reliefs with their mysteries are disturbing. The engravings on steles, obelisks and wall slabs represent beings made up of animal and human

The section of the complex that is still standing is called El Castillo, the castle, although it never was a castle.

The main portal of the Castillo, with two columns topped by a monolith nine metres long.

The columns are decorated with mysterious patterns in relief. Weathering through the ages has worn them down and, unfortunately, man, too, has damaged the delicate work.

The base of the Castillo was formerly faced with polished chiselled slabs.

Four flights of steps lead from the 'sunken square' to the four cardinal points of the compass.

Remains of walls typify the architecture of the complex. The 'sunken square' is on the right.

The Temple at Jerusalem. It was often destroyed and rebuilt on the foundation walls — like the Temple at Chavín de Huantar.

The Temple at Jerusalem is not an exact rectangle today, but an irregular trapezoid. However, it was a perfect rectangle originally.

The passages cut out of the rock are three metres high. They frequently turn off abruptly at angles of 45 degrees. How was El Lanzon brought here?

My lamp illuminated the strange heads with their stylised faces that peered from all sides.

The reliefs are so finely carved that a dentist might have been practising his hobby of sculpting with a high-speed drill.

I searched every square centimetre of the wall to find a hint of an opening, a way out.

elements as identical as technical robots. We find the same
style with the same codes, whether it be on the Lanzon stele
or the Raimondi stele, on the Tello obelisk or the monolithic
wall slabs. No one will deny that countless artists were involved
and that they all came from the same school. The works at
Chavín de Huantar would be a strange business if they were
brewed up in their own juice. But was that so?

'Winged gods' proliferate in the Mesopotamian zone. They
hovered over the portals of palaces, decorated throne-rooms
and tombs; small-scale versions of them were found on the
Babylonian, Assyrian and Hittite cylinder seals with which
private and official documents were stamped in those days.
Such 'winged gods' also fluttered and hovered in the consummate artistic abstractions at Chavín de Huantar.

The indigenous highland Indian Julio C. Tello, still the most
important excavator of Chavín de Huantar, characterised the
works of art as the products of an 'extraordinary race' (2).
Some slab engravings struck him as a mixture of fish and
dragon. He recovered images with elements of dragon, condor
and man from the ruins, monsters which are reminiscent of
diagrams of machines, if looked at from the present-day point
of view. Stylised condors fly away with outspread wings,

A symbiosis of bird, animal and man = a monster.

although they have neither birds' faces, birds' eyes or beaks. They form a symbiosis of bird-animal-man monsters, surrealistic works of art from another world by an extraordinary race, as if extraterrestrials had guided the sculptor's chisel.

Whole libraries about the Chavín style have been published. After reading the majority of the books, I should like to quote:

A delight in the use of curves is characteristic of Chavín. Powerful curves like these are not found in any other major Peruvian style. (14)

In its extremely complicated depictions of animals Chavín achieves a degree of perfection and refinement that is unknown in the human representations. The reliefs reveal a mastery bordering on virtuosity. Large hard stones are covered with a maze of elegant supple lines which look like pen-and-ink drawings. (15)

The intricacy and sophistication ... the strength and quality of the curving lines, in short, the entire concept, indicate that we are far from the beginnings of an art which doubtless evolved in other media than from megalithic sculpture. (17)

Why did such great religious artistic styles

originate in Mesoamerica
and Peru (Chavín) and not
elsewhere? What unleashed
this genius? I do not know.
(16)

The massive columns and heads of their sculptor colleagues
corresponded to the pen-and-ink drawings of the engravers.
The American archaeologist Wendell C. Bennett (18) found
two dozen heads, part human, part animal, all ornamented
with the engravings typical of Chavín. Originally the heads
protruded from the temple walls on tenons. Only two of them
are in their original place today.

The heads vary in character. Sometimes they have broad
noses and swollen lips, sometimes a rectangular animal muzzle
showing Dracula teeth snarls below the nose, at other times the
heads have no faces at all. Many are equipped with technical
accessories such as helmets, ear protectors, mouth filters and
what seem to be spectacles. A feature common to the faces
is a hostile, strange, alienating, cold expression.

Bennett also excavated megalithic slabs with ornaments that undoubtedly have value as evidence, but without human or animal features. Their sinuous lines are repeated side by side with the abstract-cum-figurative images. For all our intelligence we have not yet deciphered this symbolic language. However that is a commentary on us, not on those ancient sculptors who entrusted *their* messages to the stones, using *their* techniques.

We should not make too much fuss about the man–animal combinations — they occur in all ancient civilisations — were it not for the fact that the delicate style of the ornamentation at Chavín de Huantar is adhered to uniformly and so has more to tell us than we think. The visitor is forced to suspect that the artists did not know what they were depicting, in spite of their absolute mastery of shape and form. Did someone 'dictate' that they had to engrave? Were they using their own imaginative capacity when they immortalised the unknown something that came down from heaven in their drawings and adumbrations of jaguars and condors? When they drew their stone portraits, were they remembering the helmeted gods who gave them autocratic commands and hostile looks?

When the biblical Enoch and Elijah ascended into heaven, tradition has it that they departed on fire-breathing horses. Our ancestors knew that horses cannot breathe fire or fly. They were more familiar with four-legged creatures than we are. They probably symbolised or described the unintelligible by invoking the power of the horse as a symbol of the explosive energy of an alien phenomenon. The winged jaguars and condors meant the same to the artists at Chavín de Huantar as the winged fire-breathing horses did to the Mesopotamians and the intricate pictorial compositions originated because of the beings resembling humans who careered through the sky. In other words, they were not surreal in the artistic sense of the word, but attempts to reproduce what they had experienced.

In the book of the Old Testament prophet Job (40 and 41), we find the perfect example of a 'hippopotamus', except that it was not and could not have been such a creature, for:

His bones are tubes of bronze, his limbs like bars of iron ... His sneezings flash forth light, and his eyes are like the eyelids of the dawn ... Out of his mouth go flaming torches; sparks of fire leap forth. Out of his nostrils comes forth smoke, as from a boiling pot and burning rushes. His breath kindles coals, and a flame comes forth from his mouth ... When he raises himself up the mighty are afraid; at the crashing they are beside themselves. Though the sword reaches him, it does not avail; nor the spear, the dart, or the javelin. He counts iron as straw, and bronze as rotten wood ... He makes the deep boil like a pot; he makes the sea like a pot of ointment. Behind him he leaves a shining wake; one would think the deep to be hoary. Upon earth there is not his like, a creature without fear.

Strong meat, panegyric of a technically equipped 'Hippo-potamus'!

Old Testament scholars ascribe Job's speech and God's answer to Egyptian and Babylonian sources. Unknown creatures were lauded. The reliefs at Chavín also served as a perpetuation of actual experience.

It is just as if the Andean artists had read the Sumerian Epic of Gilgamesh (20) which contains, as part of the literary tradition, a hybrid being of the kind they symbolised in stone.

Gilgamesh and Enkidu climbed laboriously on to the top of the mountain where cedars in great profusion surrounded the dwelling of the gods. The sacred tower of the Goddess Jrnini shone forth, blindingly white.

Each of them carried an axe. Enkidu swung his and felled one of the cedars. Then a wrathful snorting was heard: 'Who was there, felling cedars?' Chimbaba himself saw them approach. He had claws like a lion, his body was covered with scales of bronze, on his feet were the talons of a vulture, on his head the horns of the wild bull; his tail and member for procreation ended in snakes' heads ... They shot their arrows at him, they hurled their throwing sticks. The weapons rebounded, he was unharmed.

Scholars claim that Chavín de Huantar was a place of pilgrimage, the religious centre of a mysterious people who suddenly appeared in the valley of the river Mosna and stamped the whole area with their culture for several centuries

— a view which the scholar Friedrich Katz (10) expresses as follows:

> Most researchers believe in a religious impulse, the emergence of a new cult which spread throughout large areas of the Andes. Many scholars believe that Chavín and perhaps the other centres of this culture were important religious towns which became the goals of pilgrimages. Afterwards the pilgrims would have broadcast the news of the new religion in the most remote villages. Even today we can still find centres of belief and pilgrims who cover hundreds or even thousands of miles to visit holy places.

In his investigation of the Chavín problem, Gordon R. Willey (21) comes to the same conclusion: 'Chavín is very obviously a great ceremonial centre,' a view shared by Julio C. Tello.

Now all religions have originators or founders. The Israelites of the Old Testament worshipped God, the Lord who created Adam and Eve, protected Noah and spoke to Abraham and Moses. The New Testament groups parables and theories about Jesus. Buddha and Mohammed also founded religions. Wherever religions originated, they have to be ascribed to semi-divine figures. Peoples were never captured by religions as the result of mass enlightenment. There were always beings, personalities, who lived among mankind or figures who set an example of what they preached.

The Chavín cult had no founder. It would be blasphemous to name jaguars, condors or snakes as the potential founders of a religion, just because we cannot root out some enlightened person.

There are scholars who connect the animal–human cult with shamanism. Shamans were the magicians who could send their souls out to the spirits or allow them to enter their own bodies. Nigel Davies (22), who has lived in Mexico for 20 years, writes:

> Anyone who escapes unharmed from a tiger in the forest is considered as one of God's chosen vessels by the Mojos (an Indian tribe in east Bolivia, EvD) and initiated into the guild of jaguar shamans. The Mojos still have a temple cult devoted to this divinity.

There is no doubt that shamanism is widespread among primitive races. We can also appreciate that the simple children of nature wanted to possess the characteristics of animals — the speed of a jaguar, the snake's cunning, the bird's ability to fly (a dream dreamt by all peoples). It is a platitude that animals were sacrificed to propitiate them. Primitive artists would never have credited wild animals with abilities they had not actually seen. Snakes crawl on the ground, but cannot fly; the jaguar runs and leaps, but cannot fly; the condor has not got legs adapted for leaping like the jaguar. It is as simple as that.

Religions and cults have laws and moral doctrines. Were they founded by jaguars, married to a shaman? Did condors spew down pious dogmas from above? And — the height of insanity — were there animal architects who built Chavín de Huantar so that they would have their own religious centre?

Assuming that the Chavín cult really was a jaguar–condor religion, would not those skilled artists have taken special care to portray their admired, feared and *revered* animals as accurately as possible? Then we should surely be able to admire perfectly realised animals on the stone monuments of Chavin, sculpted as magnificently as the sacred Apis bulls and lions of the Egyptians and Babylonians? Could not we expect to find a mummified jaguar or condor at Chavín de Huantar, since the Egyptians mummified millions of the sacred falcons of their sun god Re? Not a single mummy of a sacred animal was found at Chavín de Huantar.

What kind of god was the temple dedicated to? He could fly like a condor and also looked like a jaguar; he killed like a snake, yet had human features. He had the intelligence of a clever ruler. What kind of a god was it that combined all these characteristics?

Earlier researchers dated the building of the temple to between 1,000 and 700 BC. The theologian and historian Siegfried Huber (9), who lived in the Andes for a long time, writes:

If we can date its origins to 850 BC, Chavín emerges as the oldest, maturest art style in form and technique ... On that assumption foreigners would have come to the country around 850 BC and induced the indigenous population to accept their ideas.

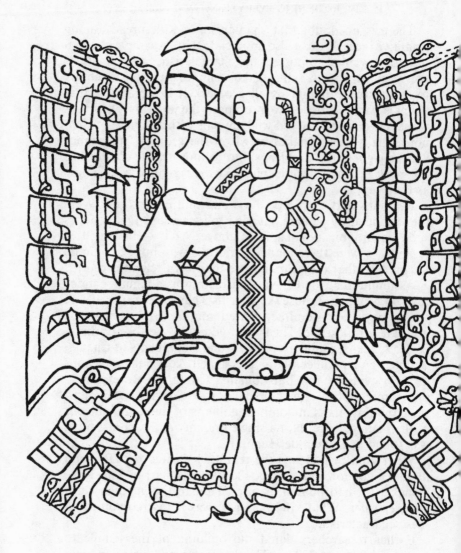

Recently scholars consider the culture to be far more recent. Peruvian archaeologists assume that it began between 800 and 500 BC. Nothing is certain, but all the dating methods in use today allow 200 years' latitude either way. Present-day physics offers modern techniques of dating ancient remains, but doubts about the dates remain.

Since an interest in archaeology is fortunately 'in', it may be of interest to say something about the techniques used for datings.

Datings are calculated by radioactive half-lives. A half-life is the period in which half the number of isotopes in a radioactive element disintegrate. A fixed value is necessary as starting-point. With the well-known carbon 14 method, the earth's atmosphere is taken as a constant with the unchanging amount of radioactive carbon isotopes. In the course of the earth's history the number of carbon isotopes reckoned to be constant was subject to fluctuations. We do not know why, but in the meantime there is no doubt that the datings are questionable.

Another point is what kind of physical artefacts are to be dated. In the same temple the shreds of a cloth and the remains of a wood fire can both be examined. What does that mean if the rags belonged to a temple dancer who practised her art in a temple that was already ancient? Nor do the carbon remains say anything about the age of the temple; the fire might have been lit in a ruined temple.

Modern physics offers eleven methods of dating, but they seldom provide clearcut dates. Each method has its snags. Analyses can often be made on specific materials and presuppose a knowledge of local peculiarities which are often unknown.

For example, microanalysis presupposes a knowledge of how high the concentration of nitrogen, fluoride and uranium was on the site in the past! Who can possibly say that with certainty? In the potassium–argon method the result stands and falls by the knowledge of the quantity of argon that penetrated (and was lost from) the stone during thousands of years. Amino-acid analysis has the weakness that it can only be used on objects that were preserved at constant temperatures, because chemical reactions alter at higher temperatures. Nobody can know whether the object to be examined was exposed to higher temperatures at some time. Temples burnt down and were rebuilt on the ruins. So every method has its faults.

Professor Richard Burleigh (23), a specialist in dating methods, holds out hopes for the future:

> The next major advance seems likely to depend on the successful development of the particle acceleration method … This method of dating, using only milligram quantities of sample offers the possibility of obtaining results more rapidly than present methods, with a probable upper age limit of about 100,000 years. Cost is likely to restrict these installations to a few fortunate institutions.

But there is one snag about this procedure; the apparatus is too expensive. Given the official lack of interest in mankind's prehistory shown by governments, limited budgets would not allocate a penny to purchase it. Perhaps the technologists should combine to invent a time machine which would let them travel back into the past. Our eyes would pop out of our heads!

The correct dating of Chavín de Huantar should lie somewhere between 1,000 and 500 BC.

Archaeologists specialising in South America point out that the equally puzzling Olmec culture originated in Mexico at the same time. It is true that the Olmecs, indigenous inhabitants of the Gulf of Mexico, did produce works of art which often resemble the Chavín style. Pottery of this kind was found at Monte Alban, a Zapotec religious centre, as well as at Veracruz and Tlatlico on the edge of Mexico City. The Olmecs' stone monster heads have similarities to their unknown brothers at Chavín, save that these comrades, which today are on parade in the museum park of La Venta near Villahermosa, are very much larger. In the Museo Nacional de Antropología in Mexico City one can see stone Olmec snake heads with technical attributes which could stem from Chavín. So has the Chavín culture got a counterpart?

I do not want to get involved in the academic battle (24, 25, 26) about which culture influenced which, but I must point out that Chavín de Huantar is in the South American Andes and not in Central American Mexico. Given a latitude of 200 years for the 'copyright' dates, it is not impossible that groups

These stone Olmec works of art (above and overleaf), which might have come from Chavín de Huantar, are on show in the Anthropological Museum in Mexico City.

of Chavín people migrated northwards or sailed there by sea and influenced the Olmecs. There are no insuperable barriers between Peru and Mexico, but there were enough incentives to make the Chavín migrate, for example in order to spread their outstandingly successful religion. Religion has always favoured adventurous excursions. Just imagine all that could have happened in 200 years that were full of gaps!

On the whole specialist literature holds the view that America was settled in a southerly direction starting from the north, present-day Canada. In his book *Kasskara and the Seven Worlds* (27), Josef Blumrich used dates and facts to prove that this drive from north to south did not exclude other possibilities. There are many South and Central American datings that are older than the North American ones, just as, vice versa, archaeologists discovered artistic evidence in the north that is older than southern artefacts.

On his plates in the Book of Mormon, Nephi tells us that he brought the record of his people's past from overseas. On his arrival, he had a temple built 'after the manner of the temple of Solomon'. Chavín de Huantar suggests itself.

There is a simple answer to the question why Nephi did not build near the coast, rather than choosing a site in the high Andes. After the landing he quarrelled with his brothers:

> But behold, their anger did increase against me, insomuch that they did seek to take away my life. Yea, they did murmur against me, saying: Our younger brother thinks to rule over us; therefore, now let us slay him, that we may not be afflicted because of his words. For behold, we will not have him to be our ruler; for it belongs unto us, who are the elder brethren, to rule over this people.
>
> (II Nephi 5.2 *et seq.*)

The outcome of the conflict was preordained. 'God' advised Nephi to depart, along with his followers. Nephi obeyed:

> And we did take our tents and whatsoever things were possible for us, and did journey in the wilderness for the space of many days. After we had journeyed for many days we did pitch our tents.
>
> (II Nephi 5.7)

No matter where the immigrants landed, they must have found themselves in country bordering on the Andes, and that was desert, genuine desert, with the exception of the few fertile strips by the river. Journeying 'in the wilderness' could only mean that the Nephites turned towards the mountains, because elsewhere there was no wilderness. And what better protection for the refugees than in the mountain valleys?

In foreign countries greenhorns find their bearings from watercourses which necessarily lead to their sources. And 'God' was always there. Nephi noted this, and also that this god could fly. He ordered Nephi, his chosen one, to 'make other plates; and thou shalt engraven many things upon them that are good in my sight.'

The connection of the builders of Chavín de Huantar with the sea is undeniable. Mussels and mother-of-pearl artefacts have been found high in the mountains.

Nephi is supposed to have reached South America around 590 BC. He had the temple built 30 years later. The complex at Chavín is dated to between 80 and 500 BC, or at the most between 1,000 and 600 BC.

Nephi knew Solomon's temple from personal observation. There were some highly educated families among his followers, as he mentions in I Nephi. Perhaps among them there were architects familiar with the temple plans.

When Nephi left Jerusalem, the city was presumably occupied by the Babylonians. In 586 BC Solomon's temple was completely destroyed by Nebuchadnezzar's soldiers. A speculation that is not too far-fetched is that the plans of the sacred temple were smuggled out of the country so that it could be rebuilt in all its glory on a new site — as a memorial to the ancient homeland and symbol of the ancient faith.

The temple complex at Chavín de Huantar can certainly have been a copy of Solomon's temple:

Chavín de Huantar has outer and inner courtyards, consecrated areas, a sanctuary (El Castillo), separate sections for pilgrims, priests and high priests, a temple wall with external rooms for the 'unclean' and even the little brook mentioned in the Bible ... everything as it was in Solomon's temple.

Chavín de Huantar was orientated towards the four cardinal points of the compass ... like Solomon's temple.

In Chavín de Huantar the number seven was looked on as sacred ... as it was in Solomon's temple.

Chavín de Huantar was a sanctuary, religious centre, and place of pilgrimage ... as was Solomon's temple.

Chavín de Huantar had a ventilation system in its windowless shrine (El Castillo) and its inner rooms had artificial lighting ... as did the Holy of Holies in Solomon's temple.

Chavín de Huantar is built over underground galleries and water conduits ... like Solomon's temple.

The builders of Chavín de Huantar worshipped a flying god ... like the Israelites.

The last statement will arouse opposition. The Israelites worshipped only the one 'ineffable' God. He was the Israelite God, who descended amid fire, noise, quaking and stench, as expressively described in the Old Testament. It was this God who ordered Moses to set bounds about the sacred mountain so that the people would not perish if they broke in:

And mount Sinai was wrapped in smoke, because the LORD descended upon it in fire; and the smoke of it went up like the smoke of a kiln, and the whole mountain quaked greatly.
(Exodus 19.18)

There was also the Israelite God's ban on making images:

You shall not make for yourself a graven image, or any likeness of anything that is in heaven above, or that is in the earth beneath, or that is under the water of the earth.
(Exodus 20.4)

According to this commandment, there should have been no representations of the gods in Solomon's temple. Was the order complied with (and at the same time got round) by making abstract images of God, as at Chavín de Huantar? Even the Old Testament confirms that Solomon tolerated other gods besides his own:

Now King Solomon loved many foreign women ... concerning which the LORD had said unto the people of Israel, 'You shall not enter into marriage with them ... for surely they will turn away your heart after their gods. Solomon clung to these with love. He had seven hundred wives, princesses, and three hundred concubines; and his wives turned away his heart. For when Solomon was old his wives turned away his heart after other gods; and his heart was not wholly true to the LORD his God, as was the heart of David his father.
(I Kings 11.1 *et seq.*)

We shall never be able to prove that his temple was also decorated with abstract representations of strange gods, because the temple was totally destroyed by the Babylonians in 586 BC. When it was rebuilt, the Roman Emperor Titus Flavius had it burnt down again in AD 70. Were images of the gods in relief or stone sculptures destroyed in the conflagration? The presence of human-cum-animal depictions of the gods in this restricted geographical zone speaks in favour of their existence. The Babylonians produced many fine examples. As did Chavín de Huantar.

As a candidate for Nephi's temple, Chavín de Huantar has more similarities to the Solomonic temple in Jerusalem than can be explained as coincidences. I found them on my excursion which was intended to put me on the trail of Ezekiel's temple.

Ezekiel's report is unique. It is like a case for private detectives. A case for Heinrich Schliemann.

Let us take a look at it!

3   A Case for Heinrich Schliemann

'The fact that things happen means nothing. It is all important that they are known.'

Egon Friedell (1878–1938)

Heinrich Schliemann's great revelation came one summer evening when a drunken man came into his father's grocer's shop in Neubuknow and gave a Bacchanalian recital of Homer's poetry. The drunk had been to a secondary school, a fact he used to remember when befogged by alcohol. Fifteen-year-old Heinrich Schliemann did not understand a word of the Homeric hymns from the *Iliad* and the *Odyssey*, but the 'music' enchanted him. He wanted to learn the language.

The gods put obstacles in his path. If the young lad had not injured himself by carrying heavy loads and so made himself unfit for manual work, he would certainly have been destined for the same boring life that his father led in the little Mecklenburg town. Heinrich signed on as a cabin boy on a freighter — the dream of all adventurous young lads. The ship was wrecked and the young sailor was saved and stranded in Amsterdam without a penny. Fortunately he found work as a bookkeeper in a business house. He had a successful career. In his spare time he learned languages. He mastered Dutch, French, English, Italian, Spanish and Russian. Because of his linguistic ability he was given increasingly important positions, especially in Russia.

During the Crimean War which France, England and Turkey waged against Russia from 1853 to 1856, Schliemann first looked after the Amsterdam firm's interests in St Petersburg, but soon founded his own business and made a sizeable fortune. He travelled in Europe and the Orient until his hour came in 1868. He settled in Athens and learnt ancient Greek. In five months he could read Homer in the original; in two years he knew Homer's *Iliad* and *Odyssey* by heart.

With Homer in his head and money in the bank, Schliemann decided to take the traditions dating back to the second millennium BC at their facè value, not just as the imaginings of a great poet. When he published his ideas in 1869, archaeologists burst their sides with laughter.

From 1870 to 1872 Schliemann excavated in Asia Minor at Hissarlik, which he looked on as the Troy described by Homer. He showed the archaeologists how literally tradition should be taken by his incredible finds. Schliemann uncovered nine superimposed settlements, including the old Homeric Troy, the citadel of which was destroyed by fire in 2,000 BC. Gold and silver treasure was found. Potsherds proved that the potter's wheel had existed there. With the seventh layer of settlement Schliemann came across signs of the Middle Bronze Age (c. 1800 BC). Walls and towers made of squared stone blocks stood on a diameter of 200 m; the inner rooms rested on circular terraces. Mycenean pottery proved to be imported, as Homer described it.

On the second layer Schliemann laid bare the ruins of the magnificent citadel of Priam and Hector, which was destroyed by Agamemnon, as Homer stated.

Schliemann the amateur gave the signal for a new look at archaeology. Convinced that Homer's poetry contained historical sources of tradition in full detail, he discovered the pre-Homeric world of the second millennium BC. Schliemann alone must be credited with giving the starting signal for prehistoric research in the Mediterranean countries. He gave the gold treasures of Troy and the royal tombs at Mycenae, and the gold treasure of King Priam, over 4,000 years old, to the Berlin Museum for Prehistory and Early History.

Scholars hid behind the dubious designation of the 'science of the spade' and claimed boldly that Schliemann had been lucky. Lucky? One man took the old traditions literally and became the greatest researcher of all time.

Heinrich Schliemann, who had latterly been the recipient of the highest academic honours, was buried in Athens on 4 January 1891.

If a Heinrich Schliemann existed today, I would have a good tip for him.

I suffer from stress every time I start to write a new book. When I realised my situation — even as I write this — I ask

myself: what is this stress we are always talking about nowadays?

I took from my library a book by Hans Selye called *Stress
beherrscht unser Leben* and learnt from the man who discovered and christened stress that this contemporary
phenomenon is not really an illness, but the body's way of
adapting to the conditions in which we live. 'Stress need not
always be harmful; it is simultaneously the root of life, for
every emotional and physical activity causes stress. The very
stress that makes one man ill may be quite stimulating to
another!' On that basis I am definitely one of the other men.

Hans Selye, the 'father of stress', wrote in his introduction
that his book was intended for both doctors *and* laymen. Consequently he felt forced to include passages that laymen could
not understand and at the same time provide explanations that
were axiomatic to doctors. He got out of the dilemma by
prefacing each chapter with a resumé which the specialist could
skip, but which would make everything intelligible to the
layman.

The problem that faced Hans Selye, born in Vienna in 1907
and since 1934 Professor of Endocrinology at Montreal, of
writing *one* book for both doctors and laymen, is very like
the difficulty I face of not being repetitious to readers who
already know my books, and yet making them intelligible to
new readers. Readers aged 20 were only five years old when
my first book came out. Encouraged and instructed by Selye,
I have marked a few pages with a black line in the margin.
My old readers can skip them. They know the texts about
the prophet Ezekiel from my books *Chariots of the Gods?*
(1969) and *In Search of Ancient Gods* (1974).

Without these quotations new readers would have no idea
what a time bomb is ticking away in the new enquiry into
the Ezekiel mystery.

Ezekiel was an Old Testament prophet. The following report
has as its subject an event that is supposed to have happened
about 592 BC.

Now it came to pass in the thirtieth year, in the fourth
month, on the fifth day of the month, as I was among the
captives by the river of Chebar, that the heavens were

opened ... And I looked, and behold, a whirlwind came
out of the north, a great cloud, and a fire unfolding itself,
and a brightness was about it, and out of the midst thereof
as the colour of amber, out of the midst of the fire. Also
out of the midst thereof came the likeness of four living
creatures. And this was their appearance; they had the likeness of a man. And every one had four faces, and every
one had four wings. And their feet were straight feet; and
the sole of their feet was like the sole of a calf's foot: and
they sparkled like the colour of burnished brass ... In the
midst of the living creatures there was something that looked
like burning coals of fire, like torches moving to and fro
among the living creatures; and the fire was bright, and out
of the fire went forth lightning ... Now as I beheld the living
creatures, behold one wheel upon the earth by the living
creatures, with his four faces. The appearance of the wheels
and their work was like unto the colour of a beryl: and the
four had one likeness and their appearance and their work
were as it were a wheel in the middle of a wheel. When they
went they went upon their four sides: and they turned not
as they went. As for their rings, they were so high that they
were dreadful; and their rings were full of eyes round about
them four. And when the living creatures were lifted up from
the earth, the wheels were lifted up ... And when they went,
I heard the sound of their wings like the sound of many
waters, like the thunder of the Almighty, a sound of tumult
like the sound of a host; when they stood still, they let down
their wings. And above the firmament over their heads there
was the likeness of a throne, in appearance like a sapphire;
and seated above the likeness of a throne was a likeness
as it were of a human form ...'

(Ezekiel 1.1 *et seq.*)

Then the Spirit lifted me up, and as the glory of the LORD
arose from its place, I heard behind me the sound of a great
earthquake; it was the sound of the living creatures as they
touched one another, and the sound of the wheels beside
them, that sounded like a great earthquake ...

(Ezekiel 3.12)

And I looked, and behold, there were four wheels beside
the cherubim, one beside each cherub; and the appearance of

the wheels was like sparkling chrysolite. And as for their appearance, the four had the same likeness, as if a wheel were within a wheel. When they went, they went in any of their four directions without turning as they went, *but in whatever direction the front wheel faced the others followed without turning as they went.* And their rims, and their spokes, and the wheels were full of eyes round about ... *And when the cherubim went, the wheels went beside them;* and when the cherubim lifted up their wings to mount up from the earth, the wheels did not turn from beside them. When they stood still these stood still and when they mounted up, these mounted up with them ...

(Ezekiel 10.9 et seq. — my italics)

I read out the last text during an extremely heated discussion after a lecture and said that it came from the Bible. An indignant opponent shouted that I should be ashamed to say that. I took *Die Heilige Schrift des Alten und des Neuen Testaments*, Stuttgart, 1972, the so-called Zurich Bible, out of my briefcase. There is no finer German version. I handed it to the enraged heckler and he shut up like a clam. The quotations preceding it also came from the Zurich Bible. [Translator's note: English version used here.]

I was just as astonished when I first came across these passages, but was immediately convinced that they seemed too technical to be interpreted in purely theological terms.

I boldly asserted that Ezekiel, or whoever wrote the first and oldest version, had seen and described a machine that suddenly came out of the clouds and understandably made a strong impression on him. Although he was eloquent, he could only stammer. He had never seen a machine before and so could not understand the functions of the wheels and wings; to him they were the limbs of 'living creatures', because they moved. Naturally the 'four wings' (rotors) were lowered when the helicopter landed. The law of gravity saw to that. The eye-witness was astonished by wheels and rings, and amazed that he was raised from the ground together with the 'living creatures'. It is a characteristic of helicopters that they take passengers with them when they take off.

Our local reporter Ezekiel heard an incredible noise. In an attempt to describe it, he could only write of 'tumult like the sound of a host' and the 'sound of many waters'. The people could imagine something expressed in those terms. He was an accurate observer; he even saw the pilot sitting on 'the likeness of a throne'.

Now the modern technical version of the text is not lacking in convincing comparisons. It was obvious to me that Ezekiel had not had a vision, but was describing a technical reality. I was given a rare bashing by the critics for my audacity because I could not prove my claims and Bernard Shaw himself said that critics are bloodthirsty people who have not had to face the hangman. But proof came from a top technologist who originally set out to disclose my assumptions as sheer nonsense.

It was a milestone in the thousands of years of biblical exegesis when an engineer analysed the texts critically. That engineer was Josef F. Blumrich, former leader of the group for constructional research with NASA at Huntsville, Alabama, the holder of numerous patents for building large rockets and the NASA Exceptional Service Medal. In his book *The Spaceships of Ezekiel* (1), he supplied an engineer's proof of the existence of Ezekiel's spaceship in the distant past. In his foreword Blumrich writes that he really wanted to prove the untenability of my theory, but he had to admit defeat, although the effort turned out to be richly rewarded, fascinating and enjoyable. These are the result of Blumrich's investigations:

It is possible to infer the general appearance of the spaceship described by Ezekiel from his account. Then an engineer can set aside his report and reconstruct a flying machine with the same characteristics. If he then shows that the result is not only technically possible, but also practical and well thought out in every respect, and moreover finds details and processes in Ezekiel's account that tally perfectly with his own conclusions, one can no longer speak simply of indications. I discovered that Ezekiel's spaceship has very credible dimensions:

Specific impulse	I_{sp} —	2,080	sec
Weight of construction	W_o —	63,300	kg
Fuel for return journey	W_9 —	36,700	kg
Diameter of rotor	D_r —	18	m

Total power developed by rotor   N — 70,000 HP
Diameter of spaceship proper   D —   18 m

The conclusions reached show us a spaceship that is not only technically possible, but also very sensibly adapted for its mission. We are surprised to find a stage of technology that is in no way fantastic, but rather falls almost within the field of our present day potentialities, in other words one that is only a little way ahead of our time. In addition the conclusions show a spaceship that was used in connection with a command module in orbit round the earth. The only fantastic thing is that such a spaceship was tangible reality more than 2,500 years ago!

A splendid by-product of Blumrich's researches was a vehicle that could move in all directions constructed from Ezekiel's description. On 5 February 1974 the engineer received United States patent No. 3,789,947 for it, which was also a belated recognition of Ezekiel's accuracy as a reporter.

So I was not lying with my crazy technological interpretation, although my critics would have loved me to be wrong.

I first took an interest in Ezekiel over 15 years ago. The old gentleman would not leave me in peace. After all, his book did not consist solely of the four chapters which had stimulated my speculations about a spaceship. It has 48 chapters, crammed full of sayings, threats, commandments, prophesies and accurate reports. It is full of curiosities.

Down the centuries the Book of Ezekiel must have had countless interpretations. In a book published in 1981 (2), 270 treatises on the prophet were catalogued, quoted and commented on. Two hundred and seventy-two scholarly heads devoted years of their lives to the ancient text. Even if little new came out of the hair-splitting exegeses — all the exegetists wear blinkers — there is still keen interest in Ezekiel today. No wonder, because a time bomb is ticking away in the texts that should lead to the trail deliberately laid by the 'Lord'. Secrets have an extraordinary attraction for people.

My (brand-new) researches concern a building which could give a modern Heinrich Schliemann excavation tips just as accurate as Homer's poetry turned out to be in pointing the way to Troy.

I reveal my find in Chapter 40 of the Book of Ezekiel and close it with chapter 48.

I have taken the liberty of only including the passages relevant to my theory, and also of italicising significant points. This is not dishonesty on my part. Everyone has a Bible and can consult the unabbreviated text. I know lots of scholarly books that use quotations the sources of which are not available to the reader.

Ezekiel writes:

In the twenty-fifth year of our exile, at the beginning of the year, on the tenth day of the month, in the fourteenth year after the city was conquered ... the hand of the LORD was upon me, and brought me in the visions of God into the land of Israel, and set me down upon *a very high mountain*, on which there was *a structure like a city* opposite me. When he brought me there, behold, there was *a man, whose appearance was like bronze*, with a line of flax and a measuring reed in his hand; and he was standing in the gateway. And the man said to me, 'Son of man, look with your eyes and hear with your ears, and set your mind on all that I shall show you, for you were brought here in order that I might show it to you ...

And behold there was a wall all around the outside of the temple area, and the length of the measuring reed in the man's hand was six long cubits, each being a cubit and a handbreadth in length; so he measured the thickness of the wall, one reed; and the height, one reed. Then he went into the gateway *facing east*, going up its (*seven*) *steps* ... Then he measured the distance from the inner front of the lower gate to the outer front of the inner court, a hundred cubits. Then he went before me *to the north*, and behold, there was a gate which faced *toward the north* ... And he led me toward the south, and behold, there was a gate *on the south* ... Then he brought me to the inner court *on the east side*, and he measured the gate; it was the same size as the others ...

And he measured the court, a hundred cubits long, and a hundred cubits broad ... Then he measured the wall of the temple, six cubits thick; and the breadth of the side chambers, five cubits, round about the temple, and the side chambers were in three stories, one over another, thirty to each story ...

I saw also that the temple had a raised platform round about. Then he measured the length of the building facing the yard which was at the west and its walls on either side, a hundred cubits ...

Over against the threshold the temple was *panelled with wood* round about, from the floor up to the windows ... to the space above the door even to the inner room, and on the outside. *And on all the walls round about in the inner room and the nave were carved likenesses* of cherubim and palm trees, a palm tree between cherub and cherub. Every cherub had two faces ...

Now when he had finished measuring the interior of the temple area, he led me out by the gate which faced east, and measured the temple area round about. He measured the east side with the measuring reed, five hundred cubits by the measuring reed. Then he turned and measured the north side, five hundred cubits by the measuring reed ... It had a wall around it, five hundred cubits long and five hundred cubits broad, to make a separation between the holy and the common ...

Afterward he brought me to the gate, the gate facing east. And behold, the glory of the LORD came *from the east*; and the sound of his coming was like *the sound of many waters* and the earth shone with his glory. And the vision I saw was like the vision which I had seen when he had come to destroy the city, and *like the vision which I had seen by the river Chebar* ... Then he brought me back to the door of the temple; and behold, water was issuing from below the threshold of the temple *towards the east* (for the temple faced east): and the water was flowing down from below the *south end* of the threshold below the temple ...

And he said to me, this water flows toward the eastern region and goes down into the Arabah; and when it enters the stagnant waters of the sea, the water will become fresh. And wherever the river goes every living creature which swarms will live, and there will be very many fish ...

And on the banks, on both sides of the river, there will grow all kinds of trees for food. Their leaves will not wither nor their fruit fail, but they will bear fresh fruit every month, because the water for them flows from the sanctuary ...

Most scholars say that the first part of the book is an epiphany. Visions of strange flashing and sparkling chariots that descended from heaven played a large part in the literature of ancient Israel. Even Eve, Adam's wife, is supposed to have seen a heavenly chariot (3):

Then Eve looked up to heaven and saw a shining chariot come, drawn by four gleaming eagles, whose glory no one born of woman could express nor look on their face, and angels went before the chariot.

(My italics)

The heavenly vehicles which flit through the traditions do not fit into any hangar! Enoch describes 'fiery heavenly cars'; Elijah went up to heaven in a similar model drawn by 'horses of fire'. When Old Testament exegetists turned their attention to Israelite tradition, they failed to note that heavenly chariots also buzz their way through Buddhist mythology (4). The great teacher Padmasambhava used such a vehicle. Ardjuna, too, hero of the Indian epic Mahabharata (5), travels gaily through the cosmos in a heavenly chariot.

Why should it not be accepted that the gods in all the myths, religions and sects all over the world actually had such heavenly chariots? Why do scholars insist on what they call a more plausible explanation of this phenomenon?

Three academic opinions are representative of the most important interpretations. The theologian Professor J. Lindblom (6) sees 'hallucinatory experiences' in the events. His Swiss colleague Othmar Keel (7) finds 'visions', while Professor W. Beyerlin (8) interprets them as part of the ritual of Israelite religious feasts. The theologian Fritz Dummermuth (9) is alone in admitting that 'the reports in question cannot readily be explained away as natural phenomena of a meteorological or volcanic kind'; and Dummermuth even remarks in a later article in the *Zeitschrift der Theologischen Fakultät Basel* (10) that 'It is about time to take a look at things from a new point of view, if biblical research is to make any progress here.'

Bravo! It would be a step in the right direction if a comparative study of heavenly chariots was made on an international scale, if Old Testament experts sat round the round table with specialists in Indian mythology and produced their respective documents.

It is senseless to confine the global phenomenon of 'heavenly chariots' to a specific local event in Israelite territory, because *it is not true.*

The figure of the 'prophet' has undergone amazing transformations during past centuries. The prophet whose word could not be questioned became the 'visionary' and, after being called 'dreamer' and 'fantast', he became a 'cataleptic'.

Man was and is inventive and will use any tricks to avoid having to tackle the inexplicable.

The Book of Ezekiel was taken apart. Semantic experts decided that style and choice of words pointed to more than one author. The prophet was abruptly relegated to the rank of 'pseudo-Ezekiel' (11), whose book was first compiled from different texts around 200 BC. A hundred years ago, the theologian Rudolf Smend (1851–1913), a distinguished Ezekiel scholar (12), wrote: 'There can be absolutely no doubt that the account is based on a visionary experience and that the vision is in no way a form of literary expression.'

The majority of theologians now think that the Book of Ezekiel was not written by the prophet, but was more probably the joint work of redactors, who mixed ancient texts (possibly including some by the prophet himself) with later additional material.

I, too, favour this explanation. 'Ezekiel' is not an original work. Practical questions make the authorship irrelevant. It makes no difference whether Ezekiel had visions or whether the book called after him originated from ancient additional traditions. My questions go to the heart of the matter:

If Ezekiel did have a vision, what purpose did his God have in mind?

If there was no vision, which parts of the text should be rated as descriptions of reality and which as the products of imagination?

If the descriptions really were phantasmagoria, we could dismiss them as science fiction.

If the accounts prove to be based on reality, where must we look for the minutely described temple?

An unanswered question is how Ezekiel, or Mister X, reached the temple and returned to Jerusalem.

The narrator of the Book of Ezekiel writes in the first person 'I saw ... I experienced ... I heard ... I was brought ...' The use of the first person has always indicated that the writer was an eyewitness. Was the man behind the 'I', whoever he was, a liar? Fabricating to make himself interesting?

The facts show that the Ezekiel narrative must be dated to the sixth century BC, whether it is attributed to the prophet (who lived at that time) or to his disciples. It was an age of strictly orthodox faith. No writer would have dared to call on almighty God as chief witness, no one would have risked putting words into God's mouth that were untrue.

'You shall not take the name of the LORD your God in vain; for the LORD will not hold him guiltless who takes his name in vain' (Exodus, 20.7).

But if lies were served up in Ezekiel's name, why does he still retain the status of a prophet in the book of books? Even if Ezekiel was not the sole author, the original was written in the first person!

Faithful to the axiom that the accused person should be given the benefit of the doubt, I believe that Ezekiel was describing real events.

In the text he says that the hand of the Lord set him down on a *very high mountain*. There are no very high mountains in Israel.

Interpretations which say that Ezekiel was describing the Solomonic temple at Jerusalem cannot be right, because that temple is not sited on a *very high mountain*. There is nothing approaching a very high mountain in or around Jerusalem, only a few hills. Moreover, Ezekiel grew up in Jerusalem and knew the hills by name. If the Lord has set him down on a hill, he would have mentioned the hill by name, given the accuracy of his bookkeeping.

From the *very high mountain* Ezekiel saw a structure like a *city*. If it had been Jerusalem, he would have recognised his home town and mentioned it by name.

There can be no doubt that Ezekiel was not describing Jerusalem and Solomon's temple.

'*And behold, there was a man, whose appearance was like bronze ...*' Since explicit sexual characteristics were not visible,

Ezekiel's instant identification of the unknown figure as a man must have come from his facial features or the fact that women, unemancipated in those days, could not give orders.

This man had the appearance *of bronze*. Excuse me, honoured exegetists, why did it not dawn on you that this man was wearing an astronaut's suit which seemed to shine like armour to the narrator?

The stranger addressed the prophet as *son of man*. Interesting, for this mode of address implies that the man with the appearance of bronze was not a man at all and that he did not know the name of the person he was speaking to. He continues to address Ezekiel as son of man. If I landed on Mars among the little green men and one of them prostrated himself in the sand before me, I couldn't say, 'Arise, John Smith.' I would have to say, 'Man of Mars, arise.' The impersonal address son of man seems to me to be a strong indication that the alien gentleman was no timeless omnipotent God. For *he* would have known Ezekiel's name.

Sceptics may ask how an extraterrestrial, for that is what I assume him to be, knew Ezekiel's language. Just as man in all ages quickly learnt the languages of newly discovered peoples, the extraterrestrials must have observed their elected groups for some time in order to master their tongue.

Now things get really exciting!

The man with the appearance of bronze tells the prophet to take a good note of what he is going to see, *for you were brought here in order that I might show it to you.*

The key to a strange story is encoded in that sentence.

If we discard the idea of extraterrestrial cooperation, almighty God had our Ezekiel transported to a *high mountain* and made a *man like bronze* measure the temple with a measuring reed before his eyes, so that Ezekiel would have the measurements firmly stamped on his memory. The detailed description shows that the prophet took his mission very seriously. What was the point of this instruction?

Theologians take the view that God gave Ezekiel a vision of the temple so that he would be able to build it in the future. But Ezekiel's temple was never built. If God showed his chosen vessel a phantom building, it means that he did not know the future and so was not omniscient.

This is the snag. In the original form of the Ezekiel text there was no grammatical future tense! Written Hebrew was made up solely of consonants; it had no vowels. In order to facilitate reading, vowels were indicated by small dots between the consonants. The original text had the imperfect and perfect tenses, but no future. But students of theology point out that the future — if need be — grows out of the consecutive perfect. Strictly speaking, the original text of Ezekiel can be transposed into the past, the present or the future, depending on which way you want it. It was a temple; it is a temple; it will be a temple.

As scholars stick to their interpretation of the text as a vision, they naturally project the building of the temple, the exact measurements of which were known to Ezekiel, into the future. The consecutive perfect makes that possible.

If we start with the assumption that Ezekiel (or Mr X) was brought to a temple which was measured before his watchful eyes, the question arises: What was the point of this accurate measurement? The text provides the answer. The prophet was to observe everything closely, because that was why he was brought there.

In my Zurich Bible, the one I usually quote from, it says: 'For thou wast brought hither for that purpose.' The same passage in the Göttingen version (14) reads: 'For I came hither to show it to thee.'

These two translations are worlds apart!

'Thou wast brought hither for that purpose,' means that Ezekiel arrived on the spot after a journey. 'I came hither to show it to you,' means that the *man in bronze* sought out the prophet. The latter translation obviously adds weight to the idea of a vision, which theologians prefer. But in context it misses its point. Ezekiel was taken to a *high mountain* and discovered *a structure like a city*. In other words, he was confronted with a new situation. He was ordered to memorise in absolute detail all the data about rooms and walls supplied by the man in bronze.

The keen observation with which Ezekiel registered the data, allow us to assume that he noted them down on the spot. In that way, the hand of the Lord achieved its goal via the bronze-clad messenger. A hitherto unknown temple entered the annals of tradition! The data for constructing a real temple — not a visionary phantom — were to preoccupy men's brains for millennia.

The aliens, my extraterrestrials — to let the cat out of the bag again — had a good idea that sacred traditions were never lost and that they would survive wars and natural catastrophes in written or printed form. They knew that priests and exegetists would grind their teeth over the mysterious event introduced into the ancient text. They knew that at some point in the future the fiery heavenly chariots would be given a *technical* explanation.

Convinced that the real measurements of a real temple are set out in the Book of Ezekiel, regardless of whether the prophet or another author wrote it, I felt I ought to be able to find at least the rudiments of this structure, which could not be overlooked because of its size.

Let the paperchase begin!

The front of the temple described by Ezekiel was *facing east*. According to the Zurich Bible the man in bronze first measured a wall, other versions speak of a 'building' or 'structure'.

The man in bronze used a special measuring reed, which was *six long cubits, each being a cubit and a handbreadth in length*. Strange. Surely a normal cubit would have been used if the whole thing was a vision. But no, a special unit was used for the measuring. And so scholars (13) wash their hands of such absurdities:

> Given an imaginary building, it is of minor importance to know whether the normal Babylonian cubit (458 mm) or the 'royal' Egyptian cubit (525 mm) more common among the Israelites is referred to ... The description is only meant to symbolise that the sacred place differed from all others.

Correct. If it *was* a vision, it makes no difference what kind of measuring reed was used, but it wasn't a vision.

The text tells us about a four-cornered building aligned on the four cardinal points of the compass. The man in bronze measured a court that was *a hundred cubits long, and a hundred cubits broad*. Ezekial observed that 'on all the walls round about in the inner room and the nave were carved likenesses of cherubim and palm trees', and that 'Every cherub had two faces.' A cherub is defined as a semi-divine hybrid figure, half-animal, half-human. Do the beings with two faces represent flying messengers of the gods? Or flying beings like those eagles that Eve saw when she described the heavenly chariots? Were they flying jaguars or mechanical products? The question-marks remain, but cherubs are always connected with flying.

The book contains an important fact about the complex. Water, i.e. a river, flowed from below the *south end* of the temple *towards the eastern region* to end in *a sea*.

Remarkably concrete data for a vision!

Equally precise facts are given about the structure of the temple complex:

Adjoining the twenty cubits which belonged to the inner court, and facing the pavement which belonged to the outer court, was gallery against gallery in three stories. And before the chambers was a passage inward, ten cubits wide and a hundred cubits long, and their doors were on the north. Now the upper chambers were narrower, for the galleries took more away from them than the lower and middle chambers in the building.

The Göttingen Bible says that ledges of rock projected into the stories, that the stories were built in three steps and consequently were narrower than the lower and middle chambers. Hence the upper chambers were set back from the ground more than the lower and middle ones.

This is the Göttingen Bible's laconic commentary: 'This seems to imply that in view of the uneven site the whole building consisted of three sections each of which was slightly set back from its neighbour.'

The devoutest of all devout theologians must surely begin to doubt whether this was only a vision. Surely if almighty God desired to show a temple he wanted built in Israel in the future, one brilliant gleaming image would have been enough? Would he have given details of how the visionary building was orientated towards different points of the compass? Would a vision contain mundane details such as the measurements of the rooms and passages, and say how the building was stepped on the uneven ground? Would it mention a stream that flowed eastwards into the sea? The theologians themselves

I had climbed out of the labyrinth high above the main entrance. The temple complex was spread out below me.

The Solomonic Temple at Jerusalem also had an infrastructure of subterranean corridors.

Over the centuries the reliefs have lost some clarity of outline, but one can still make out robot-like beings on them.

Originally the heads protruded from the walls on tenons.

The American W. C. Bennett excavated more than two dozen very strange heads.

In the Forest of the Statues I greet a person with a frightening face.

'The Bishop' in strange surroundings.

A moon-faced monolith sits on a mossy mound. It looks just like a modern work of art.

This triangular skull lies in the grass near the Bishop, guarded by a bird of prey.

A tumulus is surrounded by 30 monoliths. In the centre there is a dolmen which could equally well be standing in France! (Unfortunately the gods did not send me sun every day, or I would have used it to take photos with more contrast.)

Two figures and two menhirs support the roof; below it stands a squat figure holding a necklace from which a skull dangles.

Sarcophagi are cut out of one block of stone like bathtubs. Nearly all of them were empty when found.

(16) reject the idea that Ezekiel could have been describing the temple of Jerusalem:

> We do not know anything about such a source in the temple from the text. For we can scarcely identify it with the waters of Shiloah that flow softly; they flow in an entirely different direction.

But Ezekiel has taken special note of this stream:

> And wherever the river goes every living creature which swarms will live, and there will be very many fish ... And on the banks on both sides of the river, there will grow all kinds of trees for food. Their leaves will not wither nor their fruit fail, but they will bear fresh fruit every month ...

No stream flowing out of Jerusalem has banks teeming with life. The fuss that theological interpreters have made about the river in their religious zeal is incredible. As everything in the Dead Sea is literally dead and there can be no question of it teeming with fish, the river described by Ezekiel is dismissed as *a vision of the future!*

In order to breathe even visionary life into the river (that did not exist in Jerusalem), translators and exegetists use two tricks. There is not a single word about the 'Dead Sea' in Ezekiel, so it has been sneaked into the translation (16):

> Furthermore 'the sea' must be called the 'Dead Sea' even in the translation, since the reference is obvious to a Jewish but not to a German reader, and a translation has little value if its meaning has to be explained in a note.

Next the second trick!

After 'the river' received a name by deliberate addition to the text, it is turned into a miraculous ecological happening in the future:

First commentary (14):

> Now Ezekiel sees a second miracle. Countless trees stand in the previously barren country round the river and transform the unfertile desert into flourishing verdant land ... the river flows with the same power down into the Jordanian depression to terminate in the salt waters of the Dead Sea

... The miracle-working waters flowing from the temple leave us in no doubt about which type of narrative this chapter drew on for its images and colours; it is the river of paradise, the waters of which gladden the city of God.

Second commentary (17):

It would be a false start to waste scholarly criticism on such fantasies.
The idea of a glorification of nature is most likely ...'

Third commentary (12):

According to this, Ezekiel's expectation that in the future the temple spring will grow into a powerful river which will irrigate the barren eastern part of Judah and even make the Dead Sea pure again is perfectly intelligible. If true divine service is to take place in the temple at some time, its barren surroundings have to turn into an orchard.

Fourth commentary (18):

Describes the stream of living water which emerges from the temple and makes the land fertile and the Dead Sea pure.

Fifth commentary (16):

In the case of such visions, why look for natural connections of such doubtful value? At all events for us Christians, provided we are not merely dry as dust textual critics, this sacred river has the significance of a divine prophecy ... we recognise in it and in its workings a delightful symbol of the blessings of the holy spirit.

Vision. Prophecy. Illumination. If we follow the commentaries, Ezekiel promised an orchard and a river that would irrigate Judah, and make the Dead Sea pure. None of that has happened. Israel is still waiting for the river of paradise and the delightful blessings of the holy spirit.
In other words, criticism should not be wasted and the whole story should be accepted as a glorification of nature.

If Schliemann had treated Homer like that, Troy would probably have remained undiscovered.

In 1889 the archaeologist Georges Perrot, together with his collaborator Charles Chipiez, used the text of Ezekiel to draw a reconstruction of the temple. The two scholars took additional descriptions from the Book of Kings.

Exact reconstruction met with difficulties when it came to the unit of measurement. Which cubit had the *man in bronze* used? The Babylonian cubit of 45.8 cm or the Egyptian cubit of 52.5 cm? Or was the cubit based on some other measurement? It really does not matter, for in any case an enormous building rose from the ground.

Perrot stumbled on one fact that should not have surprised him on careful consideration:

> If we study Ezekiel more closely, we shall see that the actual temple is described in less detail than the courts and forecourts surrounding it. Actually these outer areas should have been less important to the prophet than the sanctuary. At first sight, this disproportion is surprising, but there must be a good reason for it.

The authors came up with a paradox. They said that presumably Ezekiel did not deal with the sanctuary in detail because it was well known to the Israelites. But in fact the majority of Israelites did not go further than the outer and inner courts and so knew them better than the sanctuary, which was not accessible to everybody. Then why did Ezekiel describe the outer areas so carefully?

The theologian Rudolf Smend also attempted a graphic reconstruction (12) in the last century and was surprised that the measurements of the temple were confined to length and breadth, 'with two exceptions, which are not really exceptions (Ezekiel 40.5 and 41.8)'.

These nil returns do not surprise me. The *man in bronze* realised that not much evidence of the height would be left in thousands of years. All that mattered were the measurements of the foundation walls at ground level. But the fact that Ezekiel did not take down any measurements of heights refutes the theologians' wishful thinking that the prophet described, in his hallucinations, a building to be built in the future. Heights would have been indispensable for a future building. If the interpreters would come out of their hiding places and admit that Ezekiel recorded a real building and its measurements, the mystery would be solved.

Attempts at reconstruction constantly get confused because of the assumption by the faithful that Solomon's temple in Jerusalem must have been the model. This error produces discrepancies which Rudolf Smend freely admits:

> The remaining verses cannot possibly mean 'in the pillars of the gate' and anyway it would be absurd ... In this case the expression would also be nonsensical, because gate and hall would naturally collapse ... it seems impossible for such chambers to be by all gates, because the slaughter tables [for the religious killing of living animals — E.v.D.], from which they cannot be separated, were located at only one door, the east door ... if the burnt offerings, the sin offerings and the guilt offerings were to be slaughtered on the north side of the altar, then our passage is contradictory again.

Given an exit in the wrong position, a lot of work must have been done to fit it into the scheme of the Solomonic temple.

Like Smend, the theologian and philosopher Otto Thenius (20) was amazed by the lack of heights when he attempted a reconstruction, but also astonished by the dry exact description:

> One examines the flat description, with no adornment, of the individual measurements down to the breadth of the gates and the strength of the walls and takes into account that according to this description a ground plan, and only a ground plan, can be drawn. If we assume the description to be a figment of the imagination, we get no answer to the question why Ezekiel did not give a single measurement of height for the temple ... Of course! It was not a figment of the imagination.

The theologian Eduard Reuss (1804–91), a leading representative of historical and critical theology, had difficulties with a reconstruction:

There are insuperable difficulties regarding other elements
... the 66-cubit-high columns are suspicious to us ... in
order to find the 25 cubits of the whole breadth we must
count the thickness of the rear wall in addition to the
measurements of the passage and the watch chambers that
are not mentioned here ... What does 'doors against doors'
or 'from one door to another' mean? Are we to postulate
doors in the rear wall of the watch chambers leading to the
court?

Thenius hit two nails on the head. A ground plan can be
drawn on the basis of the Ezekiel text and there is no answer
to the question of the missing heights if we assume that it was
a vision.

Taken as a whole, the attempts at reconstruction stand on
shaky feet. Measurements and supposition — for example,
by which walls, altars and washbasins are supposed to have
stood — are taken from other biblical sources and fitted into
the Solomonic temple.

In spite of some contradictions, 'Ezekiel' supplies perfectly
practical data which give an idea of what he was shown on
the *high mountain*.

My theories:

1. The temple as described by Ezekiel did exist. Ezekiel's
descriptions — and/or those of his co-authors — are not the
product of a vision. No architectonic plan for a temple to be
erected in the future was projected in a vision.

In a vision hard facts about the terrain on which the temple
was to be constructed would have been ridiculous and indications of slopes and rocks penetrating the future temple absurd.
I think a vision which risks planting productive trees with
luxuriant fruit, trees with leaves that do not wither, by that
stream or river, borders on the grotesque. All that in the
Jerusalem area! Moreover, it is not true that the prophet
himself registered everything, the man in bronze also knew
the details. Where did he get them from?

The fact that the future is used in the biblical text for the
description, 'on the banks, on both sides of the river, there
will grow all kinds of trees for food. Their leaves *will* not
wither, nor their fruit fail,' is based on the translator's grammatical judgement.

The special cubit used by the man in bronze militates against the assumption of a vision. Ezekiel was a preacher and prophet, not an architect. He could not 'create' accurate measurements out of his conscious or subconscious mind; even the actual technique of taking measurements would have been alien to him. The temple measurements would not have existed without the man in bronze.

The use of the first person in Ezekiel's description speaks in favour of an eyewitness account. Anyone who rejects his testimony as unreal stamps the whole book as a fantastic lie.

How are our industrious exegetes going to fill this explosive vacuum?

In the Book of Ezekiel, the Ark of the Covenant is not mentioned in either the general description of the temple or the record of the sanctuary. If the Solomon's temple had been the subject of the report, the most important of all relics, the Ark of the Covenant, would certainly not have been forgotten.

2. Ezekiel was describing the temple complex of Chavín de Huantar in the Peruvian Andes.

More modest than the scholars who profess to know everything as if they had been there in 573 BC, when the prophet is supposed to have had his 'vision', I summarise more than a dozen coincidences and leave the critical reader to form his own judgement.

1st coincidence	Ezekiel was brought to a very high mountain which he did not know in a heavenly chariot. Chavín de Huantar lies on such a mountain and it was unknown to Ezekiel until his arrival.
2nd coincidence	Ezekiel saw *a structure like a city* opposite him. Archaeologists have proved that an extensive urban settlement was once located near Chavín de Huantar.
3rd coincidence	Ezekiel described a temple, the main façade and main gate of which faced east. As at Chavín de Huantar.
4th coincidence	Ezekiel' complex was constructed in three steps on three superimposed terraces — as at Chavín de Huantar.
5th coincidence	In Ezekiel's account the outer court could

be reached by three gates facing north, south and east. As at Chavín de Huantar. For the Castillo stood to the west.

6th coincidence The 'inner court' measured by the man in bronze had sides of about 50 m. My Israeli friends and I measured 49.70 m at Chavín de Huantar.

7th coincidence Four steps led from the inner court of Ezekiel's report to the four cardinal points of the compass. Exactly like Chavín de Huantar.

8th coincidence The man in bronze measures the space between the side rooms as five cubits. That works out at 2.29 m using the Babylonian cubit and 2.62 m using the Egyptian cubit. My Israeli friends and I read off 2.30 m on our tape.

9th coincidence Ezekiel saw the likeness of cherubim on inner and outer walls. As at Chavín de Huantar.

10th coincidence According to Ezekiel a river flowed from below the south end of the threshold. In present-day Chavín de Huantar the stream flows down from the south, but touches the complex at the south-east corner.

11th coincidence The water in Ezekiel's account became a river flowing to the eastern part of the country. At Chavín de Huantar the little Mosna at first flows eastwards to the town of Huycaybamba, where it joined the Rio Marañon. The Marañon originally flows in a northerly direction, but then turns exactly eastward for several thousand kilometres to the basin of the Amazon, which debouches into the Atlantic Ocean.

12th coincidence The man in bronze describes to the prophet the area where the river flows as teeming with life, the water as full of very many fish. This description fits in perfectly with the Rio Marañon and the Amazon.

13th coincidence The man in bronze praises the extra-

ordinary fertility of this region with ever-
green trees and fruits. There could be no
better description of the rich vegetation on
the banks of the Marañon and the Amazon.

14th coincidence   The sacred number '7' plays as an important at part at Chavín de Huantar as it
does among the Israelites.

15th coincidence   Ezekiel described his experiences between
592 and 570 BC. Chavin de Huantar was
built between 800 and 500 BC! Given the
latitude in archaeological dating already
mentioned, a gap of 200 years would still
allow a chronological correspondence, even
if the original text were 200 years older than
is now assumed.

16th coincidence   The man in bronze told Ezekiel that his
people had built him *a new temple here*.
Chavín de Huantar originated out of the
blue. It had no forerunners.

Far fewer coincidences stimulated Heinrich Schliemann to
excavate at Hissarlik.

To be quite fair I shall also mention data given by Ezekiel
which cannot be made to tally with those at Chavín de
Huantar. In Ezekiel the whole temple complex is square.
Perhaps Chavin de Huantar was also square originally, but
then we would need to know where its eastern border was
located, for it is unrecognisable today. Ezekiel's sanctuary
formed a square with sides measuring 50 m. This size does
not match that of the Castillo. It measures 70 by 72.90 m,
only approximately a square. The crucial point is that we do
not know if later redactors corrected the measurements in
Ezekiel's account so that they could squash the Solomonic
temple on to the vision. Professor Walther Eichrodt (14) refers
to this possibility: 'Certain stylistic peculiarities suggest that
here too [he refers to the measurements — E.v.D.], the text
was altered by someone else ...'

Obviously the wooden panelling mentioned by Ezekiel can
no longer be checked at Chavín de Huantar. Nothing is left
of wood in a minimum period of 2,500 years, even if there is
no fire. Nor could I discover any palm trees in the works of

art, unless one tried to make out these tropical growths in some of the stylisations. In my opinion, animal-cum-human representations of the kind found at Chavín de Huantar could also have been mentioned in the original text, apart from the cherubs. These then fell victims to collaborators and censors to whom such pictorial elements were inopportune. The unintelligible was left out. No wonder that the Book of Ezekiel ends abruptly.

There is still something peculiar about Ezekiel. Some years ago a press report landed on my desk. Additions to the Ezekiel text had turned up in the caves of Qumran on the Dead Sea. I wrote to all the relevant addresses in the hope of seeing the finds. All in vain. Even a well-intentioned person is bound to think that there was information in the text that had to be withheld from the public. Some of the celebrated Dead Sea Scrolls are preserved in a special hall in the Israeli Museum in Jerusalem. I do not know why the architect of this Shrine

Some of the famous Dead Sea Scrolls are housed in a special hall of the Israeli Museum in Jerusalem. The architect conceived it in the shape of a UFO. Memories of the future?

of the Book conceived it in the shape of a UFO. Perhaps he shared my ideas about 'chariots of the gods'.

I realise that I have produced no *proof* of the correctness of my theories, in spite of that large accumulation of 'coincidences'. Somewhere in the world there may be other temples that fit Ezekiel's description better than the building at Chavín de Huantar. I hope that at least I have contributed to bringing the visions of chariots and temple more realistically under the critical magnifying glass.

The man in bronze had cogent reasons for flying Ezekiel to South America.

At some time between 1,000 and 500 BC the extraterrestrials reappeared. They enticed a group of Israelites — the Nephites of the Book of Mormon — to South America. They instructed the emigrants, gave them the compass and protected them.

This group was told to build a temple in South America on the model of the temple of Solomon. The Nephites and their helpers set to work, obeying 'divine' instructions. When the temple was completed one of the 'gods' flew the man in bronze to Babylon in a shuttle craft, landing near the river Chebar where Ezekiel and other Israelites were imprisoned. The man in bronze recognised Ezekiel as the spiritual leader of the group. He flew him to Chavín de Huantar and showed him the temple recently completed by the Nephites.

What was the point of it all?

To lay trails for the future! *We are the addressees.* The extraterrestrials intended Ezekiel's descendants to discover and recognise the connections — at some time in the future. They deposited in the past a time bomb for the future.

If extraterrestrials were on the earth in Babylonian times, they must have left traces of their presence in the art and literature of the region, I hear someone complain. *But they did.* We make the mistake of not taking the traditions literally and not interpreting the works of art through the spectacles of modern technology.

I shall never forget one long night spent in my home with some archaeologists who are good friends of mine.

As I am often ill at ease in the periphery of archaeology, I asked some heretical questions. I asked what we were to make of finds which do not fit into the framework, for example with technical relics which would make nonsense of all previous assumptions? Technical finds from the earliest times? They would be looked on as a dirty trick played by some envious colleague. And then? If such a find proved to be 'not of this earth' or not fitting into an already established civilisation, scholars would keep quiet about it. There was a lot of laughter about it, but it dawned on me how irresponsible this attitude was, even in jest. Sacrosanct doctrines must not be shaken.

The man in bronze sensed this when he said to Ezekiel: 'Son of man, you dwell in the midst of a rebellious house, who have eyes to see, but see not, who have ears to hear, but hear not.'

P.S. At the beginning of this chapter, Hans Selye saved me from an attack of stress. May I quote the professor again at the end of it?

Theories are indispensable. They arouse opposition, but that has its good side, because it reveals the weak points in our conceptions and shows research the direction it must take. Even a theory that does not fit all the known facts is valuable, so long as it fits better than any other hypothesis.

4   The Strategy of the Gods

(As Seen from Colombia)

'God created men because he was disappointed with monkeys. After that he gave up experimenting.'

Mark Twain (1835–1910)

'If you come here I can help you Stop Correspondence pointless Greetings Dr Miguel Forero.'

This telegram put a full stop to a series of letters I had written over a period of months to Bogotá, the capital of Colombia.

The reason for my correspondence was an article (1), 'Indio-Kultur im Dschungel,' which I had read in *Der Spiegel* on 1 February 1981. In it I learnt that mysterious cities had recently been discovered in the Colombian jungle and that the men who built them *had known more about relations with the cosmos than we do today*. That was not a reporter's opinion, but the view of Professor Soto Holguin, who was in charge of the excavations. Archaeologists are conservative in their judgements and do not willingly stick their necks out.

That was why the news excited me. Were the men of an extinct Indian civilisation supposed to have understood more about terrestrial relations with the cosmos than the brilliant children of the second millennium AD now drawing to its close? Perhaps I could find a new building stone for my theory in Colombia.

What kind of jungle cities were they and which ancient Indian tribes had built them? I read in the article that the excavation area was cordoned off by the army. Would it even be possible to visit it? At three-weekly intervals I patiently penned these questions to Professor Soto Holguin of the *Universidad de los Andes*, whom I had never met. All my letters remained unanswered. Perhaps he had something against me. Finally I turned to Dr Miguel Forero, a lawyer, with whom

Dr Miguel Forero, a Bogotá lawyer.

I have been corresponding for years. His telegram arrived promptly. If Forero cabled me to come in person, there must be a reason for it. Soon Bogotá was included in my travel plans for South America and I arranged to stop off there on my way back from Peru.

Forero was waiting for me at the airport with his extremely bright 16-year-old son Juan Carlos. During the half-hour taxi ride to the Hilton I came straight to the point: 'Do these jungle cities exist?'

'What you are looking for is called Ciudad Perdida, the lost city. It lies in the virgin forest of the Sierra Nevada, six days' journey from Santa Marta on the Caribbean Sea.'

'Why don't we hear more about it?'

'The excavation zone is cordoned off by the army. The archaeologists want it to themselves.'

'Have you any influence with Professor Soto?'

'Not yet, but I'll soon remedy that.'

'Will it take long?'

Dr Forero said I would have to wait four or five days. Apart from Professor Soto, he would have to get in touch with the army, without whose permission I would not be allowed to visit Ciudad Perdida.

Wait four or five days? That went against the grain. Time is the only asset that cannot be preserved or increased. The sulky look on my face must have spoken volumes, for Forero thought hard about how to keep me busy in the meantime.

'San Agustín! Have you ever been to San Agustín?'

I had. I was on the point of saying 'naturally', for South America had virtually become my home of the gods. But I had only spent one day there and that was too short for a thorough examination of the village and its unsolved mysteries. I grabbed at the opportunity. That very evening I booked a flight to Pitalito, a little town 500 km from Bogotá.

San Agustín was more than a way of passing the time.

At two o'clock the next day, the Aeropesca jet landed at the airport, recently built at a height of 1,730 m. If anyone asked me for my first impressions and the special characteristic of Pitalito's taxi-drivers, I wouldn't have to hesitate for a moment. They all had luxuriant moustaches! I refuse to be swamped by the torrent of verbiage from these hirsute gentlemen and Hernandez became my driver because of his trusty-looking Land-Rover.

It is one hour's drive from the airport to San Agustín, a delightful trip through the blue-green mountain scenery. The village is only a few kilometres from the 1,550 km long river Magdalena, the largest in Colombia. It was often visible, glittering in the sunlight far below in the precipitous depths.

The modest little village would have remained unknown had it not been for the term San Agustín Culture bestowed on it because of its famous megaliths.

Hernandez was disappointed when I said goodbye to him in front of the Hotel Yalconia outside the village, because throughout the journey he had praised himself eloquently as the best guide for foreigners. Tourists usually engage guides. Hernandez did not understand that I wanted to be alone.

In 1758 the Spanish monk Juan de Santa wrote the book *Wonders of Nature* (*Maravillas de la Naturaleza*). In it he gave a vivid description of the mysterious stone statues worshipped by the Indians in the valley of San Agustín.

Ninety nine years later the Italian General Codazzi, then Head of Colombia's Geographical Commission, travelled in and around San Agustín. Codazzi was a good draughtsman and sketched 34 statues and four altars. As a trained army man, he did an accurate cartographical job. He made a plan of the whole terrain, including the statues on their correct sites.

In 1857 Codazzi stood where I now stood and was puzzled, as I was. At first he thought that the statues were petrified representatives of a 'transcendental world', then he tried to fit the stone figures into the context of a religious system, but finally he was unable to explain the meaning and purpose of the layout. He had nothing to be ashamed of, for no one since Codazzi has found the answer.

In 1892 the famous German archaeologist, geologist and traveller Alphons Stübel (1835–1904) drew more statues, which were published in 1906 in his book *Vulkanberge von Kolumbien*. This attracted the attention of other German academics.

In 1911, Karl Theodor Stöpel, the Heidelberg professor, paid a visit and had the first plaster casts of the statues made. Stöpel found that the figures were mainly made of ferrous sandstone, granite and volcanic stone. He was the first man to discover the subterranean passages at San Agustín and explore them in detail (2). This is what he wrote about them:

> The same temple is laid out with massive stone flags on either side and is covered with a large stone slab, like the preceding one. Creeping through the roots of trees I managed to gain the interior and was surprised to find a lateral passage leading in a south-westerly direction, presumably leading to the other temple, the site of which has not yet been located. I would have dearly loved to explore this passage thoroughly, but had not the time. I followed it for about 30 m, but could not persuade my companions to go any farther with me. However, in the impenetrable forest region, one can realise from holes in the ground, often several metres deep, that these temples had subterranean connections with each other.

Remarkable. Today, only about 80 years later, no one wants to know about subterranean links between temples and statues. Did they lapse into oblivion? Did they hide secrets which it was inopportune to show to the public? Is it because the passages, if they really exist, do not fit into the schema which was cobbled up in the archaeological conjurer's workshops to explain the miracle of San Agustín? At any rate, the renowned Indian scholar Felicitas Barreto, who spent some time at San Agustín, told me that there were artificial subterranean passages stretching for kilometers.

Finally, the ethnologist Konrad Theodor Preuss (1869–1938), the then Director of the Museum of Ethnology in Berlin, made the first scientific survey of San Agustín (3) in 1912. He took precise measurements of everything he saw, opened a number of tombs, examined gigantic stone sarcophagi and was astounded to find them empty:

> The directions in which the chests and their openings point are too numerous for us to be able to draw any conclusions as to the meaning of the figures, and the tombs, too, are not all in the same lengthways direction, while the position of the head of the dead persons cannot be determined for the simple reason that no traces of the skeletons remain ... We may assume that the very small number of stone tombs,

namely those fitted with stone coffins, were only intended for important persons. As I did not find the slightest trace of skeletons in them, I had to conclude that they have crumbled to dust.

That is strange, too! Either the grave robbers worked so well that they did not leave the slightest trace behind them or the dead were never buried in the sarcophagi.

The empty burial sites of San Agustín reminded me of the celebrated dolmens in Brittany. Dolmens are artificial hills characterised by massive, erect unhewn stones topped by one (or more) flattish stones. The dolmens were often heaped with earth so that they look like bulges in the landscape. Prehistorians believe that the dolmens were graves. The only snag is that no skeletons have been found inside them.

Are we on the wrong track? Were these putative graves never really graves at all, either in Brittany or at San Agustín? Did the sarcophagi conceal objects that the people of those days believed to be dangerous and so covered them with earth? Could they have been gifts from the 'gods', relics of an unknown technology? Perhaps later generations assessed the danger of the objects differently and took them from their hiding place, or grave-robbers may have recognised their great value and stole what was hidden in the sarcophagi.

Professor Preuss christened certain statues at San Agustín 'moon queen' and 'sun god'. He was convinced that the stonemasons intended to represent a 'second I' in many figures. The idea is tempting, because many statues are two-storeyed. The main figure bears a second figure on its back. The I in the I? I do not think much of the idea.

The sights of San Agustín are divided into four main sectors: the Archaeological Park with the 'Forest of the Statues', the 'Spring of the Foot Washing', and the 'Hill of the Foot Washing', the 'Hill of the Idols', an artificial horseshoe-shaped plateau, El Tablon and La Chaquira, two sites high above the River Magdalena, with statues and figures carved out of the rock. In the evening, at my hotel I was struck by a strange idea which I immediately checked on the map. I found confirmation on it.

San Agustín is the only place in South America from which waters flow in the three main directions of the Atlantic, the Pacific and the Amazon basin.

The River Magdalena, which has its source up here, ends in the Atlantic Ocean. Only a few kilometres away streams descend from the 4,700 m high Purace to join the Rio Patia which in turn finally flows into the Pacific Ocean in the Bay of Tomaco. Lastly, there are the little rivers, Rio Orteguaza and Rio Caqueta, the sources of which are near San Agustín. They meet in the Rio Yaro, which becomes the Rio Japura on Brazilian territory and flows into the Amazon. This network of rivers represents an astonishing hydrographic situation! Did this fact turn San Agustín into a place of pilgrimage?

All we need to imagine is that Indians from various regions came upstream to see where the life-giving water came from. Inevitably Indians from the Pacific, the Amazon basin and the Colombian area on the edge of the Andes must have met in the mountain valley of San Agustín! Does this 'meeting of the peoples' explain the variety of the figures in the 'Forest of the Statues' at San Agustín? Did every Indian society once sacrifice to its gods in its own way at the source of *its* river, in order to conclude with the deities a covenant guaranteeing a continuous flow of water? Perhaps Amazon Indians placed a valuable gift in a sarcophagus, and their colleagues from the Pacific stole it, buried it elsewhere or destroyed it.

That was an idea that flashed into my head over my evening whisky. The next few days were to show that it was not so stupid.

I walk through the 'Valley of the Statues'. What a variety of figures! The some 200 robot-like sculptures on Easter Island in the Pacific, with their identical dour looks, are a boring lot of dummies in comparison with the wealth of artistic ideas found at San Agustín. So far 328 monuments have been found here.

In passing I greet a person only 1.15 m high. He crouches in front of a tree-trunk, with a broad flattened nose, terrifying Dracula teeth and hands raised as if in blessing above the relief of a kind of step pyramid.

On a mossy hillock made of layers of stones rests a

This almond-eyed figure is putting an embryonic something into its mouth.

moonfaced monolith — remains of a body? — with enormous eyebrows and a muzzle once again showing four Dracula teeth, a timeless creation which would not look out of place in a modern art gallery.

An almond-eyed figure introduces an embryonic something into its mouth. Broad noses and Dracula teeth seem to have been suggested by a characteristic prototype, which has set the fashion here.

In the hot humid jungle, a stunted figure under a corrugated iron roof licks an ice cream, excuse me, pushes a titbit between his frightening teeth, his grim face peering suspiciously from under the crescent moons over his eyes.

A demonic parade of idols!

The next free-standing figure makes me withdraw my boorish remark about the parade of idols, for its official title is 'The Bishop'. More than four metres high, the human face, with its large melancholy eyes, does command respect,

Under a corrugated iron roof in the hot, humid jungle, a remarkable type appears to be licking an ice cream.

This bird of prey is eating a snake that writhes round its stomach.

but after lengthy scrutiny I could not discover anything episcopal about this stone man. The Bishop is squeezing a tiny child, whose head and hands dangle downwards. It looks as if this fine fellow's next move would be to enjoy crushing the child between his fangs. Episcopal?

Ten metres beyond this dignitary, a triangular skull peeps out of the grass. Giant eyes, giant nose, giant muzzle and giant fangs show that he belongs to an alien race. But the head has its guardian — a bird like an eagle. The haughty bird of prey is consuming a snake which is helpfully curling round its bulging belly. A symbol to show that flying beings could also cope with the most poisonous animal on the planet?

Or did the eagle with the snake bring friendly greetings from Mexico? For, according to the German ethnologist Horst Nachtigall (4), the same representation is found there:

The eagle with a snake in its beak at San Agustín has an astonishing parallel in Mexican stone sculpture. On his second Mexican expedition Dupaix [researcher in the last century — E.v.D.] found in the Hermitage of La Soledad in the valley of Oaxaca a stone about one metre square, on which the same scene of an eagle with a snake held in its claws and beak is represented ... The Mexican state coat of arms shows the same scene today.

Yes, all very fine and most interesting, but it is about 3,000 km as the crow flies from Oaxaca in Mexico, the location of an eagle with a snake, to San Agustín, the site of the other! It is possible that one culture influenced the other, that Indians migrated from one place to another, but it is also possible that these companion pieces originated because the way in which an eagle strikes a snake was once observed both in Mexico and here in Colombia.

Not far from the standing eagle figure is an imposing tumulus, surrounded by more than 30 monoliths. In the centre is a dolmen of the kind to be found in France. Two figures and two menhirs support the stone slab of the roof. The two guardians of the tomb hold clubs — or are they axes? They are helmeted and over their heads hover faces apparently carrying the roof slab while in flight. Between the guardians and the menhirs behind them, a squat figure is holding a necklace from which hangs a skull.

There are many of these massive dolmens, vast monolithic works of granite, at San Agustín. One slab, for example, 4.38 m long, 3.60 m wide and 30 cm thick, rests as if weightless on menhirs rising 2.50 m from the ground. Such weights cannot be lifted without cranes and scaffolding. The builders of the 'Forest of the Statutes' were certainly not the primitive Indians we are asked to take them for. Like the builders at Stonehenge and Carnac in France, they must have set to work with tried and tested techniques in order to move such stone monsters in mountainous country. Oh yes, one incidental point. There is hardly any granite in the valley of San Agustín! Imported? How?

Often sarcophagi formed from a single block of stone lie under the dolmens, like giant chiselled bathtubs. So I ask: Were the sarcophagi originally containers for divine figures

Massive dolmens and menhirs lie in and on the ground at San Agustin.
Such weights cannot be lifted without cranes or scaffolding. The Indians
could not have been so primitive as we think they were.

and not for aristocratic corpses? Did people hope to win the
favour of the gods by enclosing their stone reproductions in
sarcophagi?

Were they so afraid of their wrath that they imprisoned
their images deep in the earth?

Even the waiters in the hotels of San Agustín are great
propagandists for the local sights.

One afternoon torrents of tropical rain poured down from
lowering clouds. It was impossible to distinguish separate
drops; it was as if a gigantic hose was deluging the country.
The water clattered on the roofs of the dolmens, spurting back
in fountains, washing the statues as it had done for thousands
of years and rustling the leathern leaves of the tropical trees.
The ground was steaming. By soaking gravel paths I reached
the Yalconia dripping wet and sat by the fire, the heat of

which dried me off outside, while whisky warmed my innards.

Long familiar with my programme, the waiter exhorted me at all costs to include a visit to the 'Spring of the Foot Washing', stretching his arms expressively to show the size of the complex. It was an absolute marvel, a maze of channels and water basins, decorated with reliefs of animals and human faces. It was a real puzzle and he was curious to find out what I would have to say about it.

At first I did not say anything, for I was speechless when I turned my astonished eyes from a framework of planks and steps to the stone miracle below me.

Over a surface area of some 300 sq m, the flattened brownish rocks contained a complicated network of handmade channels of various widths and narrow grooves, of depressions which curved through the rock like snakes, of systematically arranged large and small basins, of rectangles and circles. Reliefs of lizards, salamanders and ape-like animals appeared on the rock and the sides of the basins.

Within my range of sight, I counted 3 rectangular main basins, and more than 30 separate engravings. The labyrin-

A small selection of the many shapes at the 'Spring of the Foot Washing'.

thine channels, through which the water is led in a bewildering play, cannot be counted, but you can observe the direction of the water. It flows, dropping from one channel into another, and continues on its way as soon as it reaches a certain water-mark. The largest basin is 3.20 m long, 1.40 m wide and 81 cm deep.

In the tourist guidebook (5), published by the Colombian National Institute for Anthropology, it says:

Everything points to the fact that this was a sacred place, probably for religious ceremonies and ritual bathing. We find three water basins of different degrees of workmanship, corresponding to a certain social hierarchy. The most richly decorated was presumably for princes and priests, the second, with less ornamentation, for other eminent personages and the third and simplest for the people.

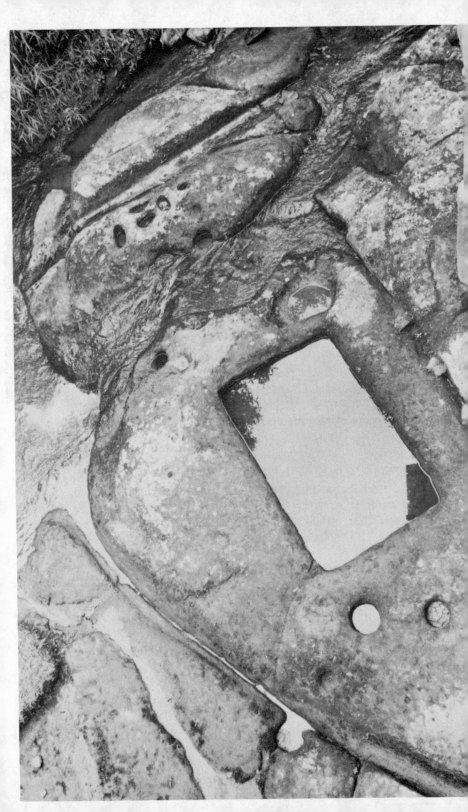

The German archaeologist H. D. Disselhoff (6) states quite boldly: It does not require too much imagination to postulate a water and fertility cult here. His colleague Horst Nachtigall (4) is a little more cautious about the purpose of the labyrinth:

Perez de Barradas [Colombian archaeologist — E.v.D.] thinks of a water and fertility cult and believes that the basins and channels must have served to receive the blood of human sacrifices, which can neither be proved nor contradicted. The significance of the complex is unknown.

That is frank speaking! How quickly archaeologists are on the spot with some cult or other when they cannot grasp something. How quickly some pedant's catalogue description leads us astray — for example the 'Spring of the Foot Washing'!

In this particular case interdisciplinary collaboration would have been a good idea. Possibly some metallurgist would have realised long ago that the arrangement of channels, furrows and basins was ideally suited to the separation and purification of molten metals of various kinds. If that could be established — and why not? — it was not foot washing that took place at San Agustin, but applied metallurgy: molten metal flowed from basin to basin, heavy particles sank to the bottom, lighter ones were carried farther, impure fragments and slag were caught in the filters of the circles and snaking grooves — a refinery built out of the rock.

The 'Spring of the Foot Washing' is not unique, a one-off achievement. I have seen a similar layout about 2,800 km away as the crow flies at El Fuerte in Bolivia.

The barren mountain peak of El Fuerte lies near Samaipata,* a little Indian village in the Bolivian jungle, five hours' drive from the city of Santa Cruz.

The mountain top resembles a pyramid made by human hands. Two parallel lines run from the bottom to the top. If we play the game 'it looks like', the images of launching ramps aligned on the heavens suggest themselves. At the upper end of the ramp, on top of the mountain, El Fuerte is flat. *And that is exactly where the 'double' of the 'Spring of the Foot*

---

* *The Gold of the Gods*, 1973; *In Search of Ancient Gods*, 1974.

A large-scale double of the 'Spring of the Foot Washing' can be found on top of the mountain El Fuerte in the Bolivian jungle.

Washing' can be found. The same labyrinth of basins, grooves, connecting channels, writhing snakes and figures, on a larger scale.

There is one suspicious difference from San Agustín. There is no spring and thus no flow of water at El Fuerte, on the highest point of the mountain, so that the wild invention of a water and fertility cult up here rapidly fades away.

Why did Indians carry out such laborious work on this mountain top?

The idea that solved the problem came not from me, but from the engineer Josef Blumrich, for many years head of NASA's Division for Project Construction at Huntsville, USA. I visted El Fuerte with him some years ago. Faced with the artificial stone labyrinth, he came up with the idea of a metal processing plant.

The pictures of El Fuerte and San Agustín speak for themselves. Whether archaeologists accept this suggestion or prefer to take refuge in a dubious cult, is not ultimately very important. But it is correct that the images prove that the cultures of El Fuerte and San Agustín had points of contact, in spite of the vast distances between them, with no roads through mountainous and tropical forests. Moreover, a water link between San Agustín and El Fuerte is conceivable. The Indians of El Fuerte could descend the Rio Mamore, which flows into the Rio Madeira, which in turn discharges into the Amazon below the present-day port of Manaus. Then the bold canoeists would have paddled up the Rio Japura to land at its source in the San Agustín region.

In spite of this theoretical link by waterways, I find it hard to believe that it was really used in practice.

The Amazon has so many tributaries to lead navigators astray that the Indian watersportsmen would have needed extremely accurate maps to reach their goal. Who could have done such hydrographic mapping in those days? Today we at last know the network of rivers in the Amazon region, but only because they were photographed by satellite from a height of 300 km.

It remains an exciting and important task to discover how the companion pieces of San Agustín and El Fuerte came into being.

I spent hours in front of and above the 'Spring of the Foot

Washing', watching tourists, who gaped at the labyrinth and certainly went away convinced that they had seen a genuine Indian footbath. The little stream of Quebrada de Lavapatas will giggle and continue to ripple past the wonder work for all eternity.

I climbed the 'Hill of the Foot Washing' up literally endless steps. The oldest archaeological traces were found up here on an artificially levelled plateau; they date back to 650 BC. This dating was taken by the carbon 14 method from the remains of wood and bones which lay on the ground around fallen statues. It cannot be established by this method whether the stone sculptures date to this period or to a much earlier one, as it is only applicable to organic finds.

Up here, on the crest of the artificially levelled hill, stands 'the Double I', *El doble yo*, incarnate in a human figure with both arms bent and hands folded over its chest. The grim face shows four fearsome fangs under the broad nose; a piercing

The 'double I' stands on top of the mountain. This figure carries an animal on its back. It stimulates the imagination to speculate why.

Yet another 'double I'. Once again a skull with enormous jaws carrying another being on its back.

look stares far into the valley from deep eye sockets. A tightly fitting helmet encloses the head.

Something after the pattern of the marsupials which were universal in the Cretaceous, the stone man carries an animal on his back — 'the double I'. Archaeology talks about a jaguar, which I was quite unable to recognise, as were other people I asked about it. A squat crest, almost as big as the head, pressed down on the rectangular skull. Does a jaguar look like that, even from a distance? Even granted the stylisation of their technique, the ancient stonemasons were closer to their subject than that.

Nearby is another figure, odder and more mysterious than its prominent neighbour. The face is carved in an abstract manner, with slit eyes above a broad mouth showing the obligatory Dracula teeth. What kind of an object this figure holds in its left hand simply baffles the imagination. The gruesome face is topped by a second 'skull', although it could equally well be something quite different.

Archaeological literature describes this monster as a 'crocodile'. I could not recognize a crocodile.

From scaffolding I examined the miracle in stone spread out at my feet.

El Fuerte also has a labyrinth of basins, grooves and channels. Was the whole site a metal-processing plant?

My stone Stone Age writer colleague.

Did idols dressed in animal skins appear at San Agustin?

The stones of Leyva: a row of twenty-four columns with others lying nearby.

A tumescent phallus 5.80 metres long. A memory of a fertility cult?

The strangest park I have ever visited.

Once again, as at Sete Cidades in Brazil, I walk over this reddish-grey honeycomb pattern formed by the cooling of the molten rock.

The model of the raft of El Dorado in the Gold Museum at Bogotá.

It is easy to find one's way in Bogotá, thanks to an intelligent road system.

With Juan Carlos in the Gold Museum. The visitor is constantly amazed by the wealth of treasures.

The four-seater Hughes helicopter flew me into the green hell.

Just before landing I took this snapshot of the topmost terrace. Could it also have been inspected from a great height in the remote past?

There is another fascinating sculpture on the plateau between the two above-mentioned figures — a monster carved out of a single block which the literature describes as a 'crocodile'. It is the first winged crocodile I have ever come across.

Even in a stylised version, the crocodile would have had long narrow jaws, not the squat muzzle that spreads almost across its head. Suppose someone tried to interpret the monster in the light of modern technology. He would recognise behind a wide open breathing apparatus (nose) two look-out holes (eyes) for pilots and to left and right the stumps of wings.

Ridiculous? If the 'gods' had inspected the Indians from a high speed shuttle craft, I would have every sympathy for the terrified stonemasons who represented the heavenly ship as a badly damaged crocodile. Even today the Papuans of New Guinea would perpetuate a landing Concorde as a being with outspread legs that plunged on to its prey with curved-down beak.

What does the 'double I' mean? As Sigmund Freud and his successors did not exist in those days, we cannot dabble in psychology or introduce schizophrenia as a solution. Those ancient artists created stylised images of what they had seen and experienced.

On the other side of the Alto de Lavapatas, the setting sun flashed from whitish grey clouds hanging deep into the valleys, gilding the grass and trees around me, while the mountains lit up on the horizon in the unreal blue of the approaching night.

An unsuspected writer colleague stood in my way, as if trying to draw my attention to trade union hours of work. Of course he was made of stone. He was getting his kicks from stereo music coming from his headphones. In his right hand, my strange colleague held a goose quill, a primitive writing tool. Or a knife which he held with the blade upwards. What else could it be? A scalpel? A flute? A blowpipe? And what was in his left hand? An eraser, if I was right about his profession. Am I right, sir, in assuming that you took down instructions from the heavenly ones? The model for this figure must have spent most of his time sitting. His short legs look stunted.

Once again sharp fangs protrude from an ugly mug. The

uniform style of the sculptors up here seems to indicate models that were not of this world, for according to my knowledge of evolution, our ancestors never at any stage had teeth of the kind that adorn a lion's mouth. My strange colleague wears lenses in front of his bulging eyes. What with the earphones and the Rex Harrison hat on his thick skull, he makes a most peculiar dwarf.

The artists who carved away up here understood a lot about representational art; they were masters of their craft. You see this everywhere in San Agustín. They made fine differentiations between men and beings resembling men, most of whom are given four monstrous Dracula teeth. Man must have been terrified of them; they left an indelible impression and that is why they constantly recur with their special characteristics. My little colleague with his tusks was certainly not of this world, either. Earphones and writing materials are strange attributes for this Lilliputian among the giants, but writers are always modest, even if they claim to receive their messages 'from above'.

The inevitable nocturnal rain tore me from my exchange of ideas with my fellow author. I rushed down the endless slippery steps, past a bamboo hedge, past images and gods who followed me enviously with their dripping eyes. They had to stick it out in the downpour; I could seek refuge by the fireside in the Hotel Yalconia. They stood out there, members of a crew of misunderstood witnesses to the remote past.

Pedro, a native tourist guide, persuaded me to conclude my week in San Agustín with a visit to el Alto de los Idolos, 'The Hill of the Idols'. I really wanted to fly home, but Pedro's enthusiasm won the day.

At the crack of dawn Pedro drove me down to the river Magdalena in the Land-Rover and then on to the Hill of the Idols. Up there the visitor finds a man-made plateau, shaped like a horseshoe, with the excavated debris sloping down from it.

It seems most likely that it was a burial ground. Horizontal stone graves, their sides formed of massive slabs, support this view, as do vertical cylindrical shaft graves and huge granite dolmens. Pedro had not exaggerated. This was a sight not to be missed.

I don't know if I am hypersensitive, but mysteries like this excite me, they fill me with awe, I sense the self-imposed mission of making my tiny contribution to the solution of the puzzle. When I see dolmens and menhirs up here on the plateau, I am immediately reminded of the dolmens and menhirs of Brittany.

Surely it is exciting that we still do not know how and why such monumental complexes were built in an unknown past? All the researchers suffer from the prejudice that modern man was the first to have an advanced technological civilisation. From that point of view the stone images made by our remote ancestors are assessed as primitive forms of expression. Yet who knows what our descendants will make of the sculptures of Henry Moore? Perhaps they will also look on them as the expression of the primitive art of our present, which will one day become the distant past.

In order to protect human life, governments and private individuals all over the world are building deep atomic shelters, primarily for survival, but also in the lurking hope that legacies of this age could provide later generations with information about our life in the second millennium.

Were the Indian tribes of San Agustín also afraid of annihilation? Did fear give them the strength to make vast bunkers underground and cover them with earth so that their refuges were unrecognisable from above? Did they want to save themselves alone or the images of the gods and their knowledge as well? I lay no claim to omniscience; I ask questions because I cannot bear being held back by scholarly taboos. Why are identical structures found in Europe and South America? What drove our forefathers to action? With elitist arrogance — our often overrated modern art may be an expression of the age — the barriers of knowledge are placed in front of the highly artistic works of the stonemasons of ancient times. But we have no right to set ourselves up as the culmination of a grandiose evolution of the human spirit. I share the views of Lao Tse, the Chinese sage, who lived around 300 BC: 'The best part of knowledge is to realise your own lack of knowledge.' But it also a continual spur to wanting to know more.

A few kilometres from the 'Hill of the Idols', just beyond the village of Isnos, I find another example of the 'double I' on the Hills of the Stones (Altos de las Piedras). This version was mentioned by Professor Preuss as early as 1913. It was accepted as fact by his colleagues, although Preuss himself was much more cautious:

> In the Mexican cultural zone we know of many gods' heads looking out of animal jaws, for example the Aztec tribal god Uitzilopochtilis looking out of the humming-bird's beak. This animal was then called the Disguise of the God and by that we understand the special form in which he may appear. Moreover it was looked on as identical with him or as his second nature. In our case, too [at San Agustín E.v.D.], we must undoubtedly look on the second head above the figure, whether it be animal or human, as a corporal extension of the main representation, as its second I. One could also postulate the heavenly nature of the god, since this second face appears above.

It is well known that primitive peoples dressed themselves in animal skins for their ritual dances, animals whose strength and characteristics they would have liked to possess. Does this trait also apply to the figures at San Agustín?

I do not know any idols, either in the original or in illustrations, that are concealed in animal skins. They do not even wear animal masks, although most of them have helmets. On close examination the bewildering ornamentation of the 'double I' — to be specific, the figure on the Hill of Stones — shows at least three faces, the third being under the rucksack with the second face, the three faces together forming a unity. Just because a dubious psychological explanation has been given, are we forbidden to ask more questions? Must Professor Preuss's theory remain in the literature unchallenged? Below I list a few ideas which offer alternatives to the prevailing opinion.

The main figure represents a priest. Above and behind him crouches the divine being who dominates him and accompanies him everywhere.

A human figure with a homunculus on top symbolises that man always has to carry the burdens of others.

The third being only emerges from the union of two beings.

The warning: man, be careful. Look out for what is happening behind your back.

The symbolisation of ancient myths which described the gods as helmeted beings, who were always accompanied by a second god. The myths say that the gods could see in all directions.

Scholars should introduce more sense or nonsense into the forest of the gods at San Agustín, so that speculation about the unsolved mystery does not come to a full stop. The helmeted figures with their excessively large teeth are certainly not meant to depict human beings. In a great many cases, the figures hold little men *without* Dracula teeth. In my view, that is how the representatives of two worlds were exhibited in stone.

Pedro had booked a friend with two horses on whose backs we rode up a steep mule-path to La Chaquira, a site high above the river Magdalena. A human figure peers from the rust-coloured rock, apparently blessing the river with outspread arms and hands raised high. *No* frightening fangs emerge from the large mouth with its swollen lips. Delicate eyebrows are in correct relation to the shape of the face, as are the eyes.

The last doubt is removed. The stone carvers of San Agustín knew perfectly well how to differentiate between human faces and the demonic masks of gods and idols.

An Aeropesca jet flew me back to Bogotá, time enough to give free rein to my imagination.

I have been a scapegoat for the academic establishment for 15 years, but I am alive and well and I don't care. What am I doing, apart from making room for imagination? It is mostly locked up in dark dungeons in our day and age. Frightened people dare not say what they secretly think.

We live in a grey age which turns people into a drab uniform product. Birds of paradise are turned into sparrows, because they are in the majority. What goes in 'King Nobel's Royal Domain' and the universities is made into intellectual currency which is internationally acceptable. Speculations about the possible and the still conceivable are eradicated. The really conceited scholars behave as if they had actually been present at prehistorical and early historical events, so brazen are their interpretations, although they cannot possibly be more than subjective impressions. In the unfertile wilderness I miss interdisciplinary collaboration between archaeologists, ethno-

High above the river Magdalena a figure stares out of the rock. It has not got Dracula teeth and the face is carved in the correct proportions.

logists and technicians of all kinds. Between the clearly demarcated areas of knowledge I am an indefatigable crosser of frontiers, I burn my fingers, I fling open the windows to let fresh air in. I know that I'm a nuisance, yet many critics should be grateful to me for the eminence they have achieved by elaborating on my successes.

We must always remember that pioneering revolutionary discoveries were made by intelligent laymen. The imaginative brain thinks something out, the scientist asserts that it is impossible and the engineer puts it into practice. People who can no longer enjoy using their imagination are condemned to a dreary monotonous path from the cradle to the grave.

My imagination works inside conceivable frameworks; I am always open to new possibilities, I enjoy refreshing associations of ideas and am grateful when I am steered off the wrong track. I am against all uniformity, especially when it comes to thinking. I look on it as sheer dictatorship if an accredited TV personality can arrange for unacceptable opinions to be banned from the small screen. The freedom to use our imaginations should be one of our acknowledged freedoms.

Apart from the exact sciences, there are literally no scientific opinions which have to be respected as facts. I take from my hand luggage the internationally respected article by Martin Knapp, 'Im finstern 20. Jahrhundert' (7) and read:

We can safely assume that many virtually unopposed 'truths' of present-day science will sooner or later turn out to be mere assertions, half-true theories, clumsy opinions or narrow dogmas. It is unintelligible why precisely today our present knowledge must be free of error or even more free of error than in the past. As in all ages men make a habit of considering themselves and their achievements as important and correct. Yet in the process each generation looks back on more errors in the past than the preceding generation. So the latest generation should be in a better position and find it more easy to decide how many errors are concealed in the present.

One textbook author writes off another with conviction. The experts quote from one another; they support their knowledge by the false achievements of others. They do not always check with the newest methods or track down contradictions in the conclusions of other fields. Last but not least, students adopt the theories of their teachers out of tactical opportunism when taking exams and often cling to them for life.

The arrogance with which many researchers, technicians and scientists represent mere theses and assertions as ultimate truth and propagate them is ridiculous and imprudent.

Dr Forero was waiting for me at the airport with such a long face that it could only mean bad news. I prepared myself for trouble.

Forero told me that he would bring a colonel in the Colombian Air Force to see me at the Hilton in the evening. The colonel knew my books and wanted to talk to me.

'Is it really necessary?' I asked.

'You want to see Ciudad Perdida, don't you? Do you want a five-day ride on a donkey on top of having to engage local guides? It's easier to let the air force take you there — in a helicopter!'

This was tempting, so I agreed to the conversation. Dr Forero had been right when he cabled that my physical presence was necessary. Contacts like this could not be made by letters.

'What about Professor Soto?'

Forero said that he had been unable to chase him up, because the head of the excavations was on the very spot where I longed to be. His office at the university did not know when he was returning to Bogotá.

I welcomed Colonel Baer-Ruiz that evening. He was of German origin and a most winning and attractive personality. Over our whiskies we talked for hours about my theories and especially about my desire to reach the 'lost city' in the jungle. I admitted that I was hoping the air force would help. I discreetly dropped the word 'helicopter' into the conversation. Colonel Baer-Ruiz knew about the archaeological discovery, but was not sure exactly where it was located. He asked for a few days' grace and then I would hear from him.

A few days' grace! Life in South America is more easy-going than in Switzerland or England. '*Mañana*' is the watchword.

All I could do was to wait for a message from Colonel Baer-Ruiz and signs of life from Professor Soto.

The day seemed endless. In the evening I accepted an invitation to dinner at the Rotary Club, which was lucky, for I met the agriculturalist Dr Jairo Gallego, a small, lively restless man like myself. I had no idea that evening of the journey my new acquaintance would launch me on. When I told him about my enforced wait, he asked: 'Do you know the Piedras de Leyva?'

I had neither heard of them nor read about them, but his description of prehistoric buildings which baffled archaeologists made me curious, especially as I thought of the wasted days ahead. Better to get to know the world and its mysteries:

> Many people only grasp
> Life's missed targets far too late.
> So, man, be wise in time,
> No time to lose, so travel, travel!
>
> (J. W. Goethe)

One could argue whether 5 a.m. is late at night or early in the morning, but it is an ungodly hour in any case. As always when my travel timetable forces me out of bed at this hour, I was amazed on this 18 May 1981 in Bogota by the considerable number of late homegoers or early risers on Carrera No. 7 outside the Hilton. I froze as I was whirled out into the cold air through the swingdoors in the foyer with my metal chests full of cameras and measuring gear. Colombia's capital lies 2,645 m above sea-level and the nights are cold there at all times of the year.

Four men, Dr Forero and his son Carlos, Dr Gallego and Carlos Esqualanta, an archaeological student, were standing round a small black Fiat.

The tight fit I was afraid of in the little Fiat turned out to be an advantage. I soon warmed up and asked cheerfully how long the drive to Villa de Leyva would take.

Dr Gallego, who sat at the steering wheel, called over his shoulder to me in the back seat, 'About seven hours!'

I suddenly found the cramped space oppressive and was already getting some idea of the numbness I would feel in feet and ankles, and later in the small of the back in two hours' time.

Gallego must have seen my horrified face in the driving mirror, for he pulled two oranges out of his pocket: 'Eat your breakfast first. The trip will fly past; I often have to do it professionally.'

The Fiat buzzed onwards. Melancholy airs came from the radio, a sound of choirs, guitars, trumpets, and a howling tenor saxophone, obviously all well-known melodies, for the two young men joined the academics in singing them. They sang all the way.

I wiped a peephole in the blurred window. Girls and boys in brightly coloured pullovers stood by the roadside; they offered painted home-fired pottery for sale, drinking vessels, beakers and basins. Heaps of stone about half a metre high made me ask if they were only road signs.

Dr Gallego said that *chicha* was served in houses with the stone piles outside. *Chicha* is a drink like beer, with a chalky colour. The South American Indians brew it under various names and from various natural products. Here among the Andean Indians it is fermented from sugar-cane or maize. The South American Indians use manioc, the albumen-bearing plant of the rain forests; they call their *chicha kashiri*.

Making home-made *chicha* is a simple business. Sugar-canes are crushed with stone or wooden cylinders. The juice is caught in jugs, heated on an open fire or glowing stones, then poured into a trough containing the remains of *chicha* from the last brew. These remains cause rapid fermentation. Indian women stir the mass, add a little water and cover the trough with banana leaves. The *chicha* is ready for drinking in 24 hours. The transformation of sugar into alcohol takes place so quickly that the brew would be ready for distilling as spirit in two days. In the case of *chicha* it must be drunk as soon as the drink is 'mature'. A day too late and Moctezuma's revenge is certain!

From the provincial capital Tunja, 2,820 m above sea level, our road led into the mountains, a primeval landscape with rust-brown and red peaks, beyond which other Andean summits could just be made out, shimmering blue and violet in the distant haze. The view reminded me of a mountain valley in Kashmir.

The valleys were traversed by the dark green strips of potato fields. Dr Gallego told me that in the market of La Paz, the highest capital in the world at 4,000 m, Aymara women offered 200 varieties of potato for sale, all cultivated in the Andes. It is archaeologically proved that Indians planted potatoes as early as the Nazca period around 200 BC and raised 625 species. Pizarro, the Spanish conqueror, introduced the potato into Europe around 1550. I realised that without Indian agriculture we should all have starved to death long ago.

The sun was blinding; it stood almost at its zenith. With engine screaming a sports car passed us on a curve with only inches to spare, followed by eight more cars obviously all indulging in an impromptu private rally. Gallego reacted in the same way as I would have done. He pulled into the side of the road until the drivers had satisfied their outburst of South American temperament.

No one had said a word. Dr Gallego changed into first gear and suggested that we eat lunch in the Hospedería Duruelo.

On the first floor of a rambling snow-white convent with its colonnades, Carmelite sisters have installed a restaurant in the refectory which outsiders can use. It is a noble room with chairs carved out of ebony and leather seats drawn up to tables covered with spotless linen, on which were bowls of orchids in all colours of the rainbow. Orchids are not expensive plants up here; they flourish like daisies do back in Switzerland.

After a brief grace, the sisters, wearing black dresses and white hoods, noiselessly served *ajiaco*, the Colombian national dish; noiselessly because they 'floated' on velvet slippers, like ministering angels. *Ajiaco* is a thick vegetable soup made of diced potatoes, peas, maize, avocados, rice and pieces of chicken. Our angels offered us cold milk and *guayaba* juice to drink. The *guayaba* is a dark-brown fruit the size of a mandarin, rich in vitamins. The Colombians claim that one glass of the bitter-sweet juice contains as much nourishment as ten bananas.

Naturally after the meal we had coffee as black as a moonless night. Wherever you go or stop or sit there is coffee. Colombians must have hearts like horses. Not only do they like coffee at any time of day and on every occasion, they are also proud of it, because it is supposed to be the only coffee in the world that is produced and exported without any chemical additive. At all events it also helps tired men on their mules.

'How much farther is it to your pile of stones?' asked Juan Carlos when we piled into the tiny Fiat again.

'Only a couple of kilometres,' Papa Forero consoled him.

And soon a rough natural path actually did lead us to the stones of Leyva. They lie or stand in a rectangular excavated area. There are no tiles or remains of walls to indicate a building to which the blocks might once have belonged, although the number and dimensions of the relics could easily have been parts of a gigantic edifice. By my measurements the rectangle was 34.40 m long and 11.60 m wide.

Twenty-four columns, the longest of them rising 3.40 m from the ground, have survived on the eastern long side. The distances between the still extant colomns allow us to calculate a maximum of 42 columns on the long side when the structure was new. In the centre of the complex some partially round

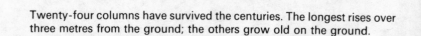

Twenty-four columns have survived the centuries. The longest rises over three metres from the ground; the others grow old on the ground.

broken columns are found. With a length of 6.80 m and a circumference of 2.75 m they pressumably towered above their other colleagues in the past.

'What was all this junk in the past?' young Juan Carlos wanted to know — he was carrying a camera for me.

'Hand me the compass, quick ...' My grey cells had clearly developed a picture I had seen!

The compass confirmed my presentiment. The rectangle is aligned on the four cardinal points of the compass, the lengthways axis running from east to west and the crossways from north to south.

The menhirs, the unhewn stones of the cromlech* at Crucuno in Brittany, are looked on as a sensation, a wonder, a mystery by archaeologists, because they are laid out rectangularly. Before this discovery, megalithic stone layouts had to be circular, as at Stonehenge, Avebury and Rollright. Stone circles can so easily be interpreted as calendars. Then came the irritating discovery of the rectangular cromlech of Crucuno, which has lain near the village of the same name in Brittany since time immemorial. The programmed interpretations began to look shaky.

There are stones there; they cannot be concealed. Twenty-two menhirs stand in an area 34.20 m long by 25.70 m wide at Crucuno; others lie prostrate on the ground and damaged; some may even have been taken away. Fernand Niel (8) showed convincingly that the Crucuno rectangle represents a calendar. The summer and winter solstices can be read off from the diagonals, the equinoxes from the lengthways axis. The rectangle formed by the Leyva stones, before which I stood, is aligned from east to west, as in Brittany.

A recognised specialist in megalithic complexes, Fernand Niel, verified that the length, breadth and diagonals of the Crucuno rectangle are in the ratio 3:4:5. This ratio is looked on as the Pythagorean or Egyptian right-angled triangle. It was a geometrical measurement in ancient Egypt.

Because the rectangular cromlech of Leyva is narrower than the one at Crucuno, other angles and diagonals result, but the number of menhirs seems to have been larger in Columbia than in Brittany.

*From the Celtic: stone circle.

Here at Leyva 24 menhirs stand on one long side. In Brittany the number is 22. In this God-forsaken place 76 menhirs must have stood guard once along the four sides — 24 on the long sides, 14 on the shorter sides. Now one cannot even guess how many columns adorned the centre.

My speculative brain was buzzing.

The more menhirs that were 'planted', the more angular calculations resulted and the more complicated the complex was for mathematical problems. A large number of menhirs also produced more lines of sight and combinations between them. Stars could be aimed at in larger numbers and more accurately. For the arrangement of the Leyva stones — as at Crucuno — clearly suggests that it was concerned with observation of the heavens. If not, why were the four rows of stones aligned directly on the four cardinal points?

I do not blame the Colombians for not trying to crack the puzzle nut of Leyva; they know nothing about its counterpart in French Brittany. We communicate all round the globe, but a distance of 10,000 km is still an unbridgeable abyss for archaeological research. Really archaeologists should be grateful for they could at least share my not inconsiderable travelling expenses when I refer them gratis to such cross-connections. They are neither grateful, nor do I see any travelling expenses. So be it. Perhaps my grandchildren will realise that their old grandpa gave quite reasonable hints in the year dot.

My young friend Juan Carlos had asked what the layout was in the past and even Forero the father and Gallego looked at me as if I was a clairvoyant for being able to give even a vague explanation on the spot. I said that I found a similarity to a famous cromlech in France and suggested that we inspect the surroundings, as we might find more information from the stones.

Only a kilometre away a tumescent penis, 5.80 m long, lay on the ground. A tree had grown through it and cracked it. Nearby was another bringer of happiness with the respectable length of 8.12 m.

Someone with a sense of humour and a bit of cheek could claim that emancipated women of the past had taken the tools out of the male workmen's hands in order to perpetuate the male sexual attribute in its most imposing state as a warning.

In many countries the phallus was a favourite subject for stone carvers, but we seldom find such fine specimens as this.

However, these symbols of sexual enjoyment did not suggest any conclusions about the geometrical rectangle.

Were they the remains of a fertility cult? Penises of this format do suggest an idea about the cult of which they formed a part. Supposing there were fixed days on which children could be conceived, or not conceived, in the immediate vicinity of the calendar stones? Did the sexologists of the Stone Age creep by and announce the happy message of female fertility limited by time? They would have had Rome's blessing posthumously. Or did giants frequent the spot to use and enjoy these enormous sex objects? Any suggestion may be viable.

I had not the slightest plausible explanation; I could only point out that the phallus was a favourite subject for stone carvers in many countries. Perhaps these phalli were only a leisure pastime for the Stone Age carvers, perhaps the same ancient psychologists — even without a couch — encouraged them to create these representations all over the world. If the archaeologists avert their prudish gaze from such finds, perhaps the sexologists could take the job on. How about a best-seller called *The Sex Life of Stone Age Man?* Ms Shere Hite, pack your bags for Leyva. You will be delighted.

The two cromlechs mentioned as aligned on points of the compass are typical examples of many similar layouts in all continents. To interpret them as calendars seems obvious, but unsatisfactory. There were simpler methods of establishing the beginning of spring and prophesying the onset of autumn.

There is something that has escaped us all so far. What are we overlooking in order to find out the secret of the Stone Age men? Crude predictions of the seasons were never needed for agriculture on our planet, because they normally occurred in a regular rhythm. A more accurate calendar would have been useful for casting horoscopes based on the stars. But seriously: did the cromlechs fix dates for the consecration of priests, for ritual festivals, for cults connected with the stars? Were such days deduced from cycles of fixed stars in the heavens? Were they monuments for visitors who came from heaven and vanished there again? In that sense, is the phallus a symbol of life that came from the cosmos? The calendar explanation may belong to the arsenal of solutions to a stone puzzle, but I do not think it is the ultimate conclusion of wisdom.

Working visits. An absurd term used for some time now by members of governments when they meet to discuss matters of mutual interest. If these gentlemen work normal hours, they are active at a 'working lunch'; if they start early, they chat away over a 'working breakfast'. Recently a European radio announcer said they had even met for a 'working drink'. In that sense, I am always busy over working breakfasts, working lunches and even working drinks while on my travels.

On the evening after my Leyva excursion, I was invited to a 'working meeting' with Swiss subjects who live in Bogotá. In this circle I met a fellow countryman, Raphy Lattion. He is Professor of Music in the Swiss College in the capital. He had read my books and so he wasted no time in asking me if I had seen the 'genetic disc'. The word 'genetic' immediately reminded me of the phalli at Leyva.

'No. What is it?' I asked.

Professor Lattion explained that a plate had been found with remarkable reliefs on both sides. On one side a series of pictures depicted the origin of life from spermatozoa to foetus, the other showed fertilisation of the cell and evolution into a frog.

'How old is the disc?'

'A few thousand years at least.'

My eyes must have betrayed my doubts; for the prehistoric inhabitants of Colombia, not being equipped with microscopes, did not know about spermatozoa. My grey-haired fellow countryman hastened to add: 'You can see the disc for yourself! It belongs to the father of a former pupil, Professor Jaime Gutierrez. Would you like to meet him?'

'Of course. Please make an appointment.'

Strictly punctual myself, I was pleased to find Professor Gutierrez waiting for me outside his bungalow on Carrera 9B, No. 126. I was impressed by his casual leisure gear, but even more so by his powerful nervous hands. They led me to think of some manual activity. I said so. A good natured twinkle appeared in the dark eyes set in the face of this tall, slim bearded man. He admitted that he was an industrial draughtsman, a subject he taught at three universities in Bogotá.

Technical-cum-artistic activity infected the whole family. In the large living room his wife, his four sons and his daughter, all over 18, as well as some friends, were all engaged in manual activity. The sons looked like replicas of Che Guevara: bearded in the manner of the Cuban doctor and guerrilla leader, and wearing the same peakless cap. When we talked, it turned out that they only shared the external attributes of the revolutionary.

All of them, girl and boys, and to some extent their mother, worked at their hobbies. They modelled or painted, made delicate mobiles. The eldest enlarged his own photos in a dark-room. Mrs Gutierrez was painting glass sheets with a fine brush, in the style of old painting behind glass. A South American family life we can hardly conceive of after the daily reports of unrest from the southernmost part of the New World. The media conceal this large part of the silent majority.

That was my first impression; the second was the showcases

Professor Gutierrez was waiting for me.

loaded with archaeological finds on all four walls, here and in other rooms. Gutierrez took Professor Lattion and me away from the family and led us into an austerely furnished study. A desk, a chair, a drawing-board and cases full of pottery and strange stones. The master of the house picked out at random an artefact like an amulet, about the size of a hand. It was covered with engraved characters.

Glozel! The word flashed through my brain.

Glozel, a hamlet like hundreds of others, is situated in the Departement of Allier between Lyons and the world-famous spa of Vichy. Glozel became famous through finds that were made there and the intrigues they fostered. Just like a detective story.

On 1 March 1924 the young farmer Emile Fradin was ploughing his fields. He was annoyed. Stones were damaging his ploughshare. So he gathered them up and piled them up at the edge of the field. While working to and fro carrying the stones, he felt that one was lighter than the others. When he removed the surface mud, he saw characters scratched on the stone that looked like T-H-O-U-X, a crazy mixture of letters. Emile Fradin put the find in his coat pocket and wiped it clean. A potsherd appeared. He could not decipher any of the engravings, but decided to sort out the potsherds from the pile of stones, because the relic could have come from the distant past. His efforts were rewarded by the discovery of hundreds of tablets and engraved stones.

The stones at Glozel were talked about as far afield as Vichy. Dr Antonin Morlet, the spa doctor, heard about them. Together with Fradin he found more stones and tablets with engravings.

Four years later, in 1928, a commission of Swedish and French authorities marched across virgin soil in Glozel, soil that Emile Fradin had not tilled. The commission found the remains of bones that were dated to 12,000 BC. The collection at Glozel was enlarged by several thousand interesting stones and some clay tablets, as well as urn-like vessels.

Quite recently the Swiss Dr Hans-Rudolf Hitz investigated the written characters and took great pains to decipher them (9). The result was as astounding as it was encouraging. The signs proved to be not only intelligible written symbols, but also rows of mathematical figures!

Drawings on the Glozel stones.

I asked Professor Gutierrez if he had ever heard of Glozel. Of course he had not; how could he? So I told him what I thought about them and asked where the stones in his collection came from.

Professor Gutierrez said that over 17 years ago he had talked to Bernardo Rincon, who was a smith by profession and had a small farm (*finca*) near Sutatausa, 40 miles northwest of Bogotá. Rincon had shown him some stones engraved with figures and characters and asked him how old they might be.

Gutierrez, who could not give an opinion, asked a geologist friend to make a rough estimate of the age of some stones and at least to decide whether they were old or young. The geologist assured him that the stones, including the engravings, were thousands of years old, because clear traces of the effects

Two examples from the Gutierrez collection; engraved stones from Sutatauso near Bogotá.

of water could be seen under the microscope. Gutierrez cheerfully told me that if I had the time and inclination, I could pick such stones out of the earth at the *finca* myself.

Was there a centre from which the stone engravings were ordered and produced? Did someone 'commission' large numbers of stones to be marked with messages and news to increase the probability that they would be found thousands of years later?

The stones at Glozel have been shown to be dated to 12,000 BC. None of the temple ruins from the Maya or Inca period, from ancient Egypt or Babylon, are considered to be as old as that. The stones must belong to a mysterious epoch much farther back than anything previously falling into the sphere of archaeology. Does archaeology not trust itself to enter this unmapped area in the history of mankind?

Finds so far reveal concentrated collections of stones in certain points in the world. As this phenomenon has not yet been systematically tackled, we can only accept the chance discoveries as a beginning, not as an end. Only after a worldwide exploration could we know if the stone plantations were holy places where the faithful deposited the precious stones, like modern *ex votos* in places of pilgrimage. Perhaps the stones had a fixed value for trading and barter, depending on the richness and contents of the engravings. Did merchants carry them in their baggage so that when they ordered goods from their suppliers they could back up the orders with valid 'currency'? Were they amulets, written communications to members of a tribe? Every interpretation has a chance — except for that of forgery. Let us admit that we have never known so little about so much as today.

Professor Gutierrez handed me a black disc, weighing about two kilos with a diameter of 22 cm and a hole in the middle like a gramophone record.

'Where did you get the disc?'

'It happened quite by chance. It is known here that I collect prehistoric and ancient objects. A few years ago a *guaquero*, a treasure-hunter, came to see me,' Gutierrez grinned: 'Perhaps he would be called a grave-robber in other parts. He offered me the disc for a small sum.'

'Do you know where the man found it?'

'*Guaqueros* have their little secrets. The man swore that it

The genetic disc.

did not come from a grave. He said he had laid a water pipe in the ground on his *finca* and found it there. He lives in the outskirts of Bogotá.'

'And the object is supposed to be old and authentic.'

Gutierrez exhaled the aromatic smoke from his black cigar through his nostrils. 'The blind feel it, those with sight see it, geologists guarantee it. This fine example of the stonemason's art is thousands of years old! Look at it. With the years the disc has been compressed by the weight of the earth it lay in. The figures were distorted, on the edges they are even pressed upwards. The symmetry of the representation of the snake is warped. In many places the reliefs have been worn down, eroded by flowing water. Two geologist friends at the Technical University confirmed what I sensed, indeed knew instinctively. The disc is thousands of years old; How many

Geologists say the disc is thousands of years old. It has been compressed by the weight of the earth so that it has been pushed upwards at the edges.

thousands I do not know. At all events they congratulated me on this magnificent piece.'

On the face, twelve ornaments divided by vertical lines run round the edge of the disc. Towards its centre is a sequence of six sectors interrupted by an arrow. Directly below the arrow are engravings of a foetus, a male and a female being, the latter clearly recognisable by penis and vagina.

'What is your interpretation, Professor?'

'At first I thought of a calendar because of the twelve divisions perhaps containing signs of the zodiac. But then what was the point of the two beings with their striking sexual characteristics? One can puzzle about the whole, but penis and vagina are unmistakable. I discussed the disc with biologists at the university ...'

'What did they say?'

'They were the men who called it the *genetic disc*. They looked at the representation from the point of view of their specialty. The biologists say that two frogs crouch directly below the arrow. A line starting to the right of the frog man runs half-way round the hole in the centre and terminates in the arrow. The line with the arrow points to the significance of the 'cartoons' on the edge. My colleagues said that they depicted the connection between vagina and penis, in other words the act of reproduction. Now follow the six fields to the left of the arrow: first field — spermatozoa; second field — male and female egg cells; third field — the fertilised egg; fourth field — the foetus; fifth field — the embryo; sixth field — the growing embryo.

'I did not understand the fields to the right of the arrow so clearly. The biologists think they might refer to an evolutionary development, perhaps on these lines: first field — cell division; second field — a water creature; third field — a batrachian, a reptile, a salamander? fourth field — possibly a bird; fifth field — an intermediate stage in the evolution towards man? sixth field — fairly obviously man. And as for the six sectors running round the centre, the three left-hand fields could represent cell multiplication, the three to the right a small woman and man — vagina and penis. Also a pregnant woman, recognisable by her breasts.'

'Fantastic,' I said and looked at Gutierrez and Lattion, who were watching me intently.

Obverse of the genetic disc.

'That's what everyone who has seen the disc says,' said Gutierrez, while Lattion asked: 'And what do you make of it?'

Careful study under a magnifying glass confirmed what the geologists had said. I spoke my thoughts aloud: 'We can forget the facile explanation that it is a forgery. I admit that the graphic, almost modern depiction of an arrow disturbed me, but arrows form part of the repertoire of all pictorial rock art. I saw arrows at Sete Cidades in Brazil, in the valleys of the Hopi Indians in the USA, in the caves of La Pileta in Spain and in Val Camonica in Italy. Arrows are stylised spears and they have existed from time immemorial.

'What can the reliefs mean? The images are too unfamiliar to be ascribed to a period so far accessible to us. The thoroughly modern conceptual ability permits us to assume that the disc has come down from a civilisation that had reached our present state of knowledge.

'The artists who created these images possessed knowledge thousands of years ahead of their time. They had the know-how which early peoples are simply not credited with. They did not possess microscopes which could have made spermatozoa or cell division visible to them, nor did they have any idea of the evolution they were representing. Did they have teachers to inform them? What do you think?'

Gutierrez pulled his beard thoughtfully. 'I could certainly imagine this disc as a teaching aid. The hole in the middle would make it very practical. The representations can be turned at will to come into one's field of vision.'

'I can only recognise the intelligible clarity of a teaching aid on the face, the obverse is pretty confusing . . .' I interrupted.

Professir Gutierrez, who has been studying the disc for years, thought that something could be read off the obverse so long as it was turned anticlockwise. As follows:

Eight o'clock: a loving couple with a symbolised vagina to the left of the man's head. Seven o'clock: spermatozoa penetrate the vagina. Six o'clock: kneeling woman with an unfertilised ovum outside the womb, with a spermatozoon floating above. Five o'clock: spermatozoa (chromosomes indicated by dots?) which lead to two ova, one ovum is empty — unfertilised — the other is fertilised. Four o'clock: the foetus. Then follow unintelligible signs, but the one o'clock

Reverse of the genetic disc.

position is obvious again: twins in the mother's womb.

'Professors must have a little left to interpret,' laughed Professor Lattion.

I thought to myself that a piece like this really belonged in a showcase in a museum, then asked, 'What do the archaeologists say?'

Gutierrez consulted several specialists about his pet piece, including Colombia's leading archaeologist, Soto Holguin. He took a long hard look at the disc, but finally admitted that he did not know what to make of it.

'Look, Erich,' said Gutierrez, 'a thing like this does not fit into any recognised plan or known culture. Where would the disc be placed in a museum? What kind of label would it be given for visitors' information? The age of the stone, and its signs, would necessitate a brand-new view of the early history of mankind. If such finds were accepted, our early ancestors could no longer be looked on as primitive hairy savages. Time is needed before a breach in the existing mental scaffolding can be made. Yes, we all need a lot of patience!'

That was true. As I was writing this, some words of Professor Hermann Oberth, the acknowledged 'father of space travel', occurred to me. 'There are scientists who behave like forcefed geese. They simply reject new ideas and concepts as nonsense.' That is also true.

Professor Oberth's statement can be quoted without need of examination. Undermining the traditional dogmas is no longer queried. Formerly churches were considered dogmatic, sciences as dynamic. The pillars of wisdom have changed their location. Today the church says that extraterrestrial, indeed extraterrestrial human life is possible ... and it does not shock the faithful. The church has long since become dynamic; it is no longer dogmatic. Science has become dogmatic and intolerant; it will not stand for opinions deviating from the currently accepted norm, except in extreme necessity. Outsiders' views can only be discussed outside 'King Nobel's Royal Domain' (10). In the process institutes and chairs for all kinds of 'ologies' multiply like rabbits. The chemist, Professor Max Thurkauf, Basle, was right when he made fun of the 'wishy-washy-wushology' in the universities.

Men of courage gladden my heart.

Professor Fred Hoyle, knighted for his service to science,

is considered to be Britain's leading astrophysicist. He has a professorship at Manchester and a guest professorship at the Caltec Technical Institute in California; he works at the observatories of Mount Palomar and Mount Wilson. By modification of the equations of the general theory of relativity, Hoyle developed a theory for a homogeneous isotropic model of the universe with the continuous production of matter.

So much for Sir Fred's scientific qualifications.

For a long time Hoyle has held the view that life came down to earth along with comet-like matter. In 1982 he took a decisive step further. He queried Darwin's theory of evolution, as well as the theory that life could have originated by chance.

I smirk; I hug myself for joy.

When I attacked this Achilles' heel of current doctrine in my book *According to the Evidence* in 1977, I was ridiculed; I was out in the open, alone in the rain. So I shall simply quote Sir Fred's ideas from his London Lecture as reported by the German News Agency on 12 January 1982.

Professor Hoyle said that man was the re-emergence of an earlier intelligence that had been faced with a universal catastrophe of cosmic dimensions. This intelligence had resolved itself into a kind of building chest, whose existential building blocks were distributed throughout the universe. All the biological basic materials from which life as we know it is composed were in this building chest. When the building chest reached the earth as a suitable environment, it developed, accelerated by additional genetic material of the kind still coming from space.

Hoyle said that on this assumption the difficulties in Darwin's theory of evolution would be obviated; it would also explain why an intelligent plan must stand behind the structures of life. For these structures are so complex that they cannot have originated by chance, as orthodox scientists claim.

With this bold statement, Sir Fred rejected two theories. First, the theory according to which life originated from a primitive soup, which created by chance processes the precisely arranged chains of amino acids on which all life depends. Secondly, Darwin's theory of natural selection, which is based on chance mutations of genes that create more highly involved plants and animals. Hoyle held the view that harmful mutations are much commoner than beneficent ones, and that consequently the process must go downhill, provided that Darwin was right.

He explained that micro-organisms were diffused throughout space in interstellar gases and that they could reach the earth in comet fragments, in whose frozen matter the micro-organisms were enclosed. Thus the arrangement of bio-materials originated by intelligent planning, not by chance.

With the favourable help of a super-technology, the intelligence would find a new material structure in which the gigantic stock of information — the intelligence — could be transmitted.

So much for this extract from Professor Hoyle's important lecture. I venture to add some of my own personal observations.

My critics trumpet that extraterrestrials were never like humans, that molecular chains on distant planets would have arranged themselves into a completely different order from those on earth, and so would have produced quite different results from our own.

That is not necessarily so. The first intelligent form of life was formed somewhere in the universe. When and where that happened is beside the point; we do not know. This intelligent form of life sent the germs of life, molecular chains or basic biological material out of its galaxy in all directions — life bombs (building chests) as I postulated in *The Stones of Kiribati*. Some containers traverse the universe, reach no goal or crash into alien suns; others come into the gravitational field of a *virgin planet*.

What happens? If the surface of the planet is unsuitable for the basic genetic material, it will die; it cannot flourish. But if it is suitable, the 'sowing' proceeds according to a coded programme. It is much the same as if the seeds of a tree flourishing in Europe are planted in Australia. If the soil there is not right, the seeds will not grow; if it is, a tree like its European forebears will grow, owing to the genetic information encoded in the cells. Much the same thing happens with Hoyle's building chests. This demolishes the problem of identicality or similarity. Wherever the cosmic seed grows, it develops in exactly the same or a very similar way to the way it did in its place of origin.

This theory does not exclude the possibility of life in the universe whose forms and appearance would exceed our wildest flights of fancy. But no such form of life would ever thrive on our planet. Critics who are already prepared to consider this theory at the same time warn that it would be absurd to admit that humanoid beings in the universe would think and act like us.

Because what I said over 15 years ago is now a burning topic, I will give a brief summary of my ideas. Alien, intelligent forms of life visited our planet thousands of years ago. They took some cells from *the already existing hominids* and changed them by genetic manipulation, a process that is already practised today. Gene technicians can already deliberately alter hereditary characteristics (GEO, February 1982). Only two years ago, the view was that planned genetic manipulations would not be possible for at least 100 years, if at all.

The genetically manipulated cell was put into a liquid culture in which it grew to the egg stage. The egg was implanted in the potential mother. (Artificial insemination of human and animals has long been practised.) The resultant child had all the parents' qualities but, owing to the genetic manipulations, it possessed additional qualities and abilities which its parents did not — for example, the ability to speak, the faculty of storing experience in the brain and to summon it up as memory at any given time. I said that the theme was burningly topical.

At one time in the USA there were trials before the high courts with evolutionists and fundamentalists as the protagonists. The evolutionists (mainly from the scientific camp) wanted confirmation that life on earth originated by chance and then developed further on the evolutionary principle (as propounded by Darwin). The fundamentalists (mostly orthodox believers) wanted the biblical act of creation confirmed. God created man in his own image.

Apart from the fact that every court requires a procedural clarification, both sides only represented a half-truth. If the opponents had taken the extraterrestrial element into consideration the conflict would have ended or not even begun. the evolutionists are right in so far as evolution, mutation and selection exist, but they do not clear up the central problem

The whole steep mountainside seems to have been piled up like a grotesque birthday cake.

'My name is Sylvia. Welcome to Buritaca 200!' a bright-eyed beauty greeted me.

From the end of the gorge a steep flight of steps with a gradient of 50 degrees led 1,100 metres up to the big terrace.

Below the excavation finds there were stone mills for grinding corn — household objects, scoops and vases.

The steep slopes of the Buritaca valley were cut into and buttressed with stone, earth and supporting walls.

Sylvia pulled aside a curtain of lianas and opened up a view of still more surprises.

What in fact was Buritaca? A city of priests? A military outpost?

of how life originated or how intelligence began. The fundamentalists are right in so far as life arrived on earth from outside and that 'God' or 'gods' formed hominids and made them intelligent in their own image. Once the extraterrestrials are drawn in, even anthropologists need not look for the missing link, which is artificial mutation by extraterrestrials.

Perhaps the genetic disc which lay before me contains the information we are looking for. In any case, I wish the archaeologists one Fred Hoyle for the next ten Christmases!

Gutierrez spread out some drawings on the desk.

'What do you think they are?'

'Pages out of your son's chemistry book.'

'They are rock drawings from the *Piedras de Tunja*, the stones of Tunja.'

'Where can I see them?'

'Forty kilimetres north-west of Bogotá.'

'So near?' I already had Tunja in mind as a place to visit, seeing that I still had a few free days to fill in. While I was studying the chemical formulae, molecular chains (for that is what they looked like), Gutierrez handed me a book (11).

'Here. The drawings are reproduced in it. The archaeologist Miguel Priana wrote about the Tunja stones as early as 1926. He assumed that they were drawings by Chibcha Indians, but I don't agree. I know a great many Chibcha works of art and this is not their handiwork. I think that the drawings stem from a much more ancient culture. We may be the addressees of the mysterious messages, once we can read them.'

Dr Forero had not been able to reach Professor Soto, nor had Colonel Baer-Ruiz shown signs of life. Forero wanted to try other possibilities of getting me to my goal. Yesterday Professor Gutierrez said that one must have patience.

I decided to go to Tunja.

Forero sent my young friend Juan Carlos to guide me out of the maze of traffic and accompany me to Tunja.

Thanks to a road map carefully prepared by his father, with all turn-offs marked in red, we left the city in a rented Chevrolet by a first-class road in a north-westerly direction, past brightly painted houses with big metal footballs on the roof. Football fans obviously showing their premature joy about the World Cup Final in Colombia in 1986.

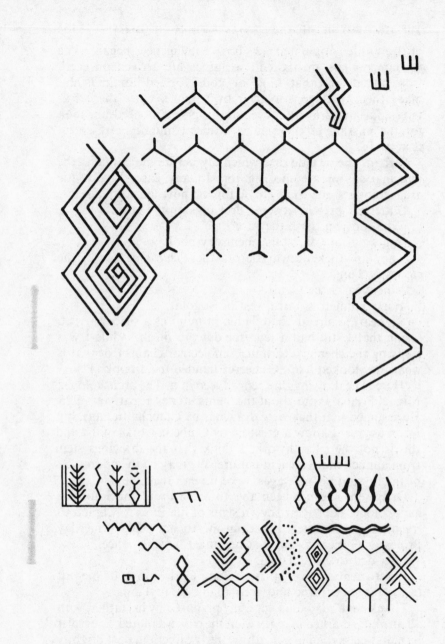

Drawings on the Tunja stones like illustrations in a chemistry textbook.

We are driving through scenery which reminds me of the Swiss Canton of Appenzell, an immaculate pre-Alpine landscape. There was activity everywhere. The land was worked intensively. Willow hedges were set up, fields ploughed, fruit and pottery were on sale; no sign of the lethargy which I observed so frequently in the highlands of Mexico and Bolivia.

In Facatativá, an eyrie with a few single-storey houses, Juan Carlos asked where the stones of Tunja were. We were told they were at the end of the village. When I parked next to the Army School, the speedometer showed 40.5 km. Gutierrez had estimated the trip very accurately.

A large sign announced that the *Piedras de Tunja* were in a government-protected zone. It said *Parque Arquelogico de Facatativá* and outlined everything that was forbidden. No fires to be lit; drive carefully and park where indicated; do not paint stones or trees with signs or scratch them with tools. All praise to the government in Bogotá!

An amazing site. Along well-kept empty roads, watched by only a few black and white cows, I strolled past colossi and square and rectangular stone blocks. They excluded any idea that nature had played eccentric games here. However prodigal she may be, nature does not make dead straight lines run round whole blocks of stone. One thinks rather of a temple frieze, a 'roof', which rested on strong columns in the past and then collapsed.

Were they relics of the legendary Masma culture, that hypothetical culture which is supposed to have existed thousands of years ago and whose traces have been suspected in all quarters of the globe?

The Peruvian geologist Daniel Ruzo introduced the concept of a Masma culture into the literature (12). He coined the concept of a putative legendary culture which left hitherto inexplicable traces. I saw them in the Peruvian Andes at a height of 3800 m, barely 50 km from the capital, Lima. They are assembled on the plateau of Marcahuasi, which has an area of about three square kilometres.

Up there Daniel Ruzo photographed statues of animals from the Mesozoic, badly eroded by weathering, among them a stegosaurus, which belonged to the dinosaur species and lived in the early Cretaceous. During his excursions, Ruzo also came across reliefs of lions and camels, which supposedly never lived in South America.

The geologist aimed his camera at various times of the day and in different seasons on the same strange rock formations of Marcahuasi and made an amazing discovery. He caught a crag with the visual outlines of an old man on the plate, but on development it showed the face of a young man.

Fascinated by Marcahuasi, Ruzo travelled the world and collected photographic proof of what he called Masma culture, for want of a better word. His stimulating book was, and is, completely ignored, although it came out in 1974.

Ruzo's photographs came into my mind during my walk through the Archaeological Park, as did the idea that keeps on nagging at me. Why do we stubbornly refuse to recognise the remains of ancient cultures in weird inexplicable rock formations? Because we all share the erroneous opinion that man never transformed rock faces into works of art?

Even people who have never been there know the monumental stone sculptures of Mount Rushmore from photographs. In the state of South Dakota, south-west of Rapid City, the gigantic faces of Presidents George Washington, Thomas Jefferson, Theodore Roosevelt and Abraham Lincoln stare out of the naked rock. Immediately next to them an eccentric artist produced his own work. Using pneumatic drills and dynamite, he sculpted the mountain face into a colossal equestrian statue of the Indian chief Sitting Bull.

The presidential heads are carefully tended, otherwise they would soon be covered with lichen and crumble away under the influence of wind and weather. Assuming that this expensive maintenance work had long since ceased, what would intelligent men read into the eroded stone sculptures thousands of years later. Would they interpret the four heads and the equestrian statue as 'geological freaks' of nature? Probably. Because no one in his right mind has overturned mountains into monuments.

Our age will not take the trouble to investigate the provenance and origin of the monoliths scattered about the stone park of Facatativá as if a giant had thrown them there. Comparative archaeology could provide a solution to what is puzzling here, to what points back to the distant past, to what lies beneath my feet in a greyish-red honeycomb pattern.

DEPARTAMENTO NACIONAL DE PLANEACION
CORPORACION AUTONOMA REGIONAL DE LA SABANA DE
BOGOTA Y DE LOS VALLES DE UBATE Y CHIQUINQUIRA

Parque Arqueológico de Facatativá

Cercado de los Zipas

LA CORPORACION SALUDA A LOS VISITANTES Y LES ENCARECE: No dibujar sobre las piedras ni prender fuego cerca de ellas, puesto que contienen pictogramas de gran valor histórico. Cuidar los árboles y la vegetación-No deteriorar las construcciones Conducir los vehículos con prudencia y estacionarlos en los lugares determinados

I trod the same honeycomb pattern in Brazil at Sete Cidades, the Seven Cities between the town of Piripiri and the Rio Longe. There as here the rock must have become molten hot like lava during a volcanic eruption. There as here nothing has moved. The heat must have been released like an explosion and then cooled down, so that the honeycomb pattern formed on the spot during the rapid cooling process. Iron became molten, oxidised and left the rust-red colour behind on the honeycomb pattern.

Facatativá and Sete Cidades became Indian holy places. Inexplicable rock drawings and engravings are found at both sites. Both places present the picture of a devastating catastrophe liberating enormous heat in which stone monsters were hurled through the air.

Indians hammered and engraved the drawings which Professor Gutierrez had shown me on massive stones beneath overhanging cliffs. In the Archaeological Park they have the special rank of the 'Stones of Tunja'.

What is the message of these engravings which look like chemical formulas? Are they signs, meant as warnings? Do they tell of a catastrophe that happened here in the past? Are they notices defining a zone that it would be dangerous to enter? For possible answers, we must take a look at some very recent experiments.

The American atomic authority NRC commissioned a research group to work out how generations living thousands of years after our time could be warned not to enter a still active atomic waste depot.

Thomas Sebeok, the head of the group, was in favour of covering the storage area with gigantic warning signs on which a communications mixture of symbols, images and words were engraved, since men would not know our language and writing thousands of years later. In addition, the experts recommended taking into account the human tendency to superstition. Hidden threats should be engraved on the signs in graphic form so that future men would think that entering the zone would evoke a supernatural revenge. *Der Spiegel* (13) added: 'As experience shows that such warnings attract rather than repel inquisitive people, Sebeok also recommended sowing the surroundings of the atomic waste depot with the vile smell of long-lasting stink bombs.'

I do not know if bombs can be produced which will still stink in the distant future, but the idea of the warning signs I find very, very dubious. What material would they have to be made of to last thousands of years? If we postulate gold or platinum, lovers of the noble long-lasting metals would certainly find them. I bet that the signs would not stay put for long.

Supposing the idea was mooted of entrusting warnings to the rocks at Facatativá? As far as possible on protected rocky summits, just as the Indians transmit their information? That seems to be the most likely explanation of all. History has proved it.

Under the threat of global annihilation a great deal of money is wasted on research and on illusionary models for saving mankind. In the same way, government bakshish has been allotted to prehistoric research. Don't we realise that the fatal situation which may confront it has been survived once or even many times? I am afraid that what Montesquieu

(1689–1755) said is true: 'Man hardly ever reaches reason from reason.'

When the Spanish conquerors overcame the highlands around present-day Bogotá in April 1538, the stones of Tunja were already worshipped as a shrine. The Spaniards encountered Indian tribes whom they called Chibcha because of their communal language. They were settled between Nicaragua and Ecuador. The Muisca belonged to one linguistic group of the Chibcha. They did not erect any monumental buildings, but they produced sophisticated pottery, were skilled in working gold and knew how to weave very fine cloth.

Why were the Tunja stones worshipped as holy relics even in those days? Here, where I was walking, the Muisca held their festivals in honour of the gods, here they sacrificed boys to appease the wrath of god. Why just here? Was it not just a place like any other? We can conclude from the traditions of the Muisca that the Tunja stones were considered sacred from the very remote past.

The sungod Chiminigagua (gagua means sun) emerges from the mists of mythology. The Spanish chronicler Simon Pedro (14) followed Indian stories in relating the arrival of the god:

It was night. As yet there was nothing in the world. Light was enclosed in a great something house and came out of it. This something house is Chiminigagua and it concealed the light inside itself, so that it came out. In the gleam of the light things began to be.

Chiminigagua, the sun or light god, was the almighty ruler of the universe to the Muisca; they saw him as a beneficent god, but they did not build temples in which he was supposed to dwell. He took his something house with him. Messengers went to and fro between the Chiminigagua and the Muisca — instructing the Indians in useful activities, teaching them morals and religion and finally vanishing, but not without announcing that they would return.

This tradition has a counterpart in the myths of the Caribes Indians. The Caribes Indians lived in the hot humid Colombian region near the northern Andes. The myths of the Caribes Indians (15) relate that mankind stems from a certain

Louquo who came from heaven, like his Muisca colleague. Firstly he created intelligent men, whom he taught to catch fish, build houses and plant manioc before he returned to heaven as a god.

Chiminigagua and Louquo, the Inca god Viracocha and the Maya god Kukulkan are at the centre of traditions which have the same message. 'Gods' came down from heaven, created men, became their teachers and finally vanished into the unknown in mysterious fashion. Their 'children' were left behind, incapable of grasping the miracle they had experienced.

The strange figures were not made into constellations, nor did stars become symbols of the vanished 'gods', until after their ascents into heaven. As the concrete visions left the earth without a trace, they obviously had to be at home 'up there', from whence they had come. It was only natural that the places in which they visibly and physically lived were elevated to the status of holy places, like the Tunja stones in the Archaeological Park of Facatativá.

On the homeward journey Juan Carlos asked, 'Do you know the story of El Dorado?'

'Vaguely. I know that El Dorado means the golden; I know that concept stands for the legendary land of gold.'

'And you don't know the Muisca mythology?'

'Do you know it?'

'Si, si, señor. We learn the story at school, and now it has even come into our home.'

'Tell me about it.'

Juan Carlos sat up straight in his seat.

His vivid account was emphasised with volatile gestures of the kind only South Americans use. 'All right. When the Spaniards came to these highlands in the sixteenth century, they showed the captive Indians gold and precious stones and tortured them to find out where similar gold and precious stones could be found. In terror of their lives and as they did not know where the treasures were hidden, they told the conquerors the traditional story. Between ourselves, Erich, they did a lot of harm.

'This is the story the Indians told the Spaniards:

'Before a new Muisca ruler could be installed, the chosen one had to spend a period of solitude in a cave. On the day of the summer solstice he made his way to Lake Guatavita, 2,600 m high in the mountains. All the members of the tribe were awaiting him up there. On the shore they had built a raft of wood and reeds, decorated with flowers and garlands. In the darkness of night they placed four bowls of burning charcoal and a lot of *moque* (incense) on the raft. Because it was a feast day, the men were adorned with feathers and the women wore their finest ornaments of gold, coral and precious stones.

'In the darkness of the night the future ruler was taken out naked, rubbed with resinoid earth and then covered with a layer of gold dust. Not one bit of his body was left uncovered, not even his hair.

'After this procedure the chosen one was led to a raft, in the centre of which he had to stand motionless. A prince was posted at each corner. I do not know if it was as magnificent a picture as the one in our school books, but it must have been a fine sight. Just think about it. The dark night, a raft, five princes on it, adorned with gold chains and earrings, at their feet mountains, literally mountains of gold and precious stones. And then when the sun crept over the mountain tops, when its first rays reached the raft, at that moment the shores of Lake Guatavita sprang to life. A great chorus of flutes, drums and song sounded from the shores and could be heard deep in the valleys.

'Slowly the raft with the five men was rowed out into the middle of the lake. And then it happened!

'The young gilded ruler brought the sungod his gifts. He threw all the treasures on board into the lake and the four princes followed suit.

'Then the raft neared the shore. The gilded one entered the lake and was washed to the accompaniment of ritual hymns. Now he was the new king of the Muisca.'

'A beautiful myth ...' I had heard it before, but could not deprive the young man of the pleasure of telling it.

'No myth, señor! It did happen. When the level of Lake Guatavita fell owing to drought, a lot of gold was found. Word of honour!'

The story Juan Carlos defended so vehemently is true.

Already in 1545 Hernan Perez le Quesada tried to lower the level of the lake. Thousands of Indians scooped water out of the lake using empty gourds and wooden scoops. Because it was the dry season and the surface level was lower than usual, it was possible to lower it by three metres, enough to recover 4,000 gold pesos.

The next attempt in 1580 failed. Antonio de Sepúlveda hired 8,000 Indians whose furious prospecting changed the face of the landscape in a way that is still visible today. On the side facing the valley, Sepúlveda had a V-shaped cut made through which the water slowly drained away. By the time the artificial gorge collapsed on to the effluent water the level of the lake had sunk by 20 m. Sepúlveda was able to send to his Christian majesty, King Philip II, in Madrid a catalogued treasure of golden breast plates, snakes, eagles, rods and an emerald as big as a hen's egg. The entrepreneur kept back 12,000 gold pesos for himself, but still died in poverty. Sepúlveda was given a tomb in the church of Guatavita, near the lake whose gold had enchanted him and brought about his downfall.

The lure of the Muisca gold persisted down the centuries. Adventurers kept on trying to empty the lake to recover the rich booty. Limited companies were formed and constructed underground channels. Gold objects were constantly brought to light, but the great majority of gold artefacts is still hidden in the depths of the lake. It appears that someone once reached the bottom, but it was covered with a layer of slimy mud 20 m deep, which even the bravest diver could not face. Pumps from Bogotá came too late. The surface of the mud became rock-hard in the heat of the sun. Then the waters covered the Muisca treasure once again. Experts estimated tht it was worth about 100 million US dollars.

A myth with tangible traces.

Who inspired the poor Muiscas to sacrifice their country's treasures to the sun god? Who spurred them on to gild their tribal prince, the man they looked on as next to the gods, for a religious ritual? Had extraterrestrials worn suits that gleamed like gold? Did the naive Indians believe that gods who came down from the sun demanded sacrifices of gold and jewels?

'Do you know the *Museo del Oro*?' asked Juan Carlos, when we were saying goodbye outside the Hilton after a nerve-racking drive through the free-for-all traffic in Bogotá. Yes, I had visited the Gold Museum ten years before. Only part of its 28,000 archaeological exhibits can be on show at any given time, so that another visit could be well worth while. We made a date for the next day which I would have to keep, provided there was no news taking me into the jungle.

The harsh ringing of the telephone awoke me at an unpleasantly early hour. Dr Miguel Forero was on the line and I was wide awake at once.

'Have you contacted Professor Soto?'

'No, that won't be so easy to do, but in the meantime would you like to talk about your theories to some air force officers?'

'Of course, I'll do anything to get to Ciudad Perdida! A lecture is OK with me, so long as one of the officers has a helicopter in his pocket.'

'How are you going to spend the day?'

'I've arranged to meet Juan Carlos in the Gold Museum.'

The Gold Museum housing Colombia's outstanding gold finds was established in 1939 by the *Banco de la Republica* in the second storey of the bank's head office at Street No. 16. It is protected by massive steel doors and guarded by armed security officers.

I am delighted to say that taking photographs is still allowed,

The treasures in the Gold Museum are protected by massive steel doors.

as it was ten years ago. In most European museums the guards become hysterical when they see a camera. You have to hand them in before a visit. The idea is that the objects on exhibition suffer from being photographed. I can understand that in the case of ancient documents constantly subjected to flash photography, but now there are highly sensitive films with which you can take pictures in semi-darkness.

I claim that archaeologists — whose museums specialise in 'hard ware' — prohibit photography for two reasons. Firstly they want their own photographs to be sold. As an author who is all for sales promotion, I find that attitude scandalous. Where do the archaeologists get the money for their researches, where do museums get their subsidies? From the tax-payer's pocket. That is why I consider it a swindle when excavated objects are held to be personal possessions. Secondly, there is a desire to prevent amateur archaeologists with cameras from interpreting objects in a way which does not fit into the orthodox theories. *All* interpretations are subjective. While unaccredited intruders are kept out of 'King Nobel's Royal Domain', it is difficult for outsiders to oppose new views to the settled sacrosanct doctrines. Louis Pauwels and Jacques Bergier wrote in their book *Aufbruch ins Dritte Jahr-Tausend* (16): In addition to the freedoms which are guaranteed us by the constitution, we should demand another one: The freedom to doubt science.'

In the darkened rooms of the Museo del Oro silence reigned. Thick carpets swallowed up the sound of one's footsteps. People spoke in whispers and were frightened when they saw a strange face reflected in the glass of a showcase. One felt reverential before the piles of primitive treasures.

The guards led us into a dark room in which soft music came from invisible speakers. Theft-proof steel doors closed behind us automatically. We tried to get our bearings and then bright lights were switched on. We were in a treasure-house crammed with gold. Works of art from every tribe of Colombian Indians hung from the walls behind heavy panes of reinforced glass. Precious objects ornamented with gold, silver and platinum hung from the ceiling.

Confused by the plethora of riches, I concentrated on individual pieces, the meaning of which was inexplicable. Both then and now precious metals were and are not used for everyday objects. They were undoubtedly religious artefacts, stylised representations of important divinities, given that artists hammered figures, faces with helmets, into the precious metal.

There are rarities from the cultural heritage of the Quimbaya Indians. The museum guidebook says: 'Anthropomorphic stylisation,' i.e. human features in non-human beings. As a child of our times I could see a robot in them; legs astraddle, something like a head and on it two capsules like the casing of two alarm clocks. There are variations on these 'anthropomorphic stylisations', sometimes decorated with wings, sometimes with rods, but the alarm clocks are always there and they give the objects a technical touch.

The Calima Indians are depicted with very large skulls and wide bony noses quite alien to their racial type. Rings almost as big as the head dangle from their ears and wide gold face masks 'drop' from their noses. Moreover helmets are crammed on to their heads, terminating in wings decorated with balls,

A smart amulet with many puzzles, I was able to solve one of them.

discs, dots and rods, yet the alarm clocks are always there too. We ought to think about who or what was symbolised here. The museum guide makes it easy; he refers to these Calima works as 'diadems'. Liz Taylor is an authority on diadems. Someone ought to ask her if she would like to deck herself out in the style of this square skull.

Then there is as elegant round amulet with a figure on it. One cannot say whether it is a man or a woman. The artist was presumably symbolising a porter. The figure holds tree trunks or stone pillars leading to the lowest point of the triangular skull and a similar feature lies across its ankles. Memories of the ancestors who suffered under the burden of stones in Facatativá?

An amulet with a figure from whose skull rays shot out also interested me. In front of its chest a disc hangs over a wide belt. The fabulous creature crouches on a litter like a throne, which is carried by two embryonic monsters (animals?). Wherever there is an empty space balls appear. Balls seem to have played an important part in the repertoire of these ancient artists.

On another breast plate, an autocratic being is being carried on a litter, but here by little stylised men. The being holds two objects, the one in his left hand might be a beaker, the one in his right hand is more technical looking. Once again balls (or discs) float round the face. The ball game so favoured by the ancient Indians dictated that the only graphical accessories they could give figures were balls, varying only in size.

It is said that the balls or discs represent sun and moon. I do not believe it. Even Pre-Columbian Indians could see that there were only one sun and one moon in the sky! Why did a plurality of these emblems dominate the pictures? I find them too prominent as pure ornamentation and besides they take up too much space. Can we assume they were the Indian's conception of the world as a sphere? Were balls (or discs) a symbol of the eternal to them?

What can have gone on in the head of the Indian artist when he placed a humanoid creature with giant frog eyes, straddling spindle legs and spindle arms in another amulet? The two birds flanking the creature seem too big in proportion to the figure. This group of three appears on a frieze which is supported by long crossed legs. Stylised in the manner of

A stylised mannikin is juggling with balls. The ancient Indians were so fascinated by balls and discs that they never depicted figures with any other adjuncts. There was a reason for this.

a cornflower, eleven balls enclose two beams below the frieze. In the lower sector of the four-storeyed representation, a little chest is included with two balls resting on its lid.

Scholars say that this amulet is a nose ring because the circle is open at the top, so that it could be clipped on to the nose. They may be correct, but then the artistic depictions would hang sideways.

And of course the Gold Museum houses some model aircraft — I'm sorry, representations of insects. All the models are low-flying, with the wings brought back under the rump and vertical tail fins. Archaeologically, these golden jewels are catalogued as 'religious ornaments', attributes of a fish or insect cult. All very well, except that there is no trace of a fish

I think these 'religious ornaments' are model aircraft and I'll tell you why.
These little jewels are behind reinforced glass so thick that my colour
photographs did not come out. In gold they look good enough to steal!

or insect cult among the Colombian Indians. Besides, the model aircraft do not have fish or insect heads.

The Gold Museum was well worth my second visit. The thousands of exhibits stimulate the imagination and make one admire the ancient Indian artists. They take one far back into the world of puzzles and mysteries, the world which was so ruthlessly ended by the Spanish conquerors.

That evening my patience snapped. Dr Forero is a kind, helpful and reliable man and I did not doubt for a moment that he was making great efforts on my behalf. Over dinner he explained to me that many of the air force officers whom Colonel Baer-Ruiz wanted to invite were away on courses or commandos and that he did not want me to lecture to a tiny audience. Dreaded *mañana* was rearing its head.

Dr Forero suggested in all earnest that I should stay in the country for another three months. A big UFO congress was due to take place in Bogotá in August and the organisers would be delighted for me to lecture. And during that time I would certainly be able to achieve my aim of visiting the lost city in the jungle. *Mañana*.

I had allowed one week for this excursion in my travel plans, after that I had contracted to give lectures in Germany, Austria and Switzerland as part of my programme for the year.

'I'm going to fly to Santa Marta and try to find my own way into the jungle,' I said. Dr Foreero advised against this.

If the army had cordoned off the excavation zone, not even a Colombian, let alone a foreigner, could reach it.

I thanked Dr Forero warmly for all his help and said I was sure we should meet again.

The next day I flew back to Switzerland.

5   The Eighth Wonder of the World

'The question today is how we can persuade mankind to agree to its own survival.'

Bertrand Russell (1872–1970)

Before my departure I had booked a room in the Hilton for 14 August. At the end of July I confirmed with Dr Forero that I would attend the congress in Bogotá, but added that my main reason for coming was to meet Professor Soto and visit the lost city.

Lufthansa flight 512 landed punctually at 21.40 hours on the rain-soaked landing strip at Bogotá. Was I dreaming? Had nearly three months passed since I had flown away from here in frustration? The certainty that I would now be able to see the lost city delighted me.

My booking was confirmed at the Hilton, the youthful head of reception told me, but there was no room available. Furious because it was night, I was tired and no other accommodation would be available, I tried the old joke.

Putting on my most serious face, I asked, 'Would you have had a room for Queen Elizabeth if she had arrived unexpectedly?'

The young man looked at me with a wild surmise. 'Well,' he said perplexedly, 'in that case we would have to make an exception.'

'Give me the Queen's room. I promise you she won't arrive tonight.'

The man in the black suit had no sense of humour. He refused to offer me one of the rooms which all hotels of this category keep in reserve. After one last question: 'So you've no room for me?' I began to open my bags so that I could lie down on a sofa in the hall. Why should I suffer for a blunder by the staff? I was worn out after the flight and the resultant jet lag; I longed for a bed. Worried about my imminent striptease, the young man summoned the manager and of course he had a room for me. Why couldn't I have had one straight away?

At nine o'clock the next morning I was woken from a long refreshing sleep. Dr Forero was on the line.

'So you're here. I can't believe it!'

'But we did arrange to meet today.'

I had arrived before my letter written at the end of July. We met an hour later. Apart from three lectures in the Teatro Libertador, I was to address the Rotarians on two evenings and also give the talk which Colonel Baer-Ruiz had planned during my last visit.

'What news of Professor Soto?'

Miguel Forero was prepared for my question and took a book from his briefcase entitled *Buritaca 200 (Ciudad Perdida)*, the Lost City (1). The author: Professor Soto Holguin. I flicked through it. Flights of steps overhung with lianas, moss-covered walls, terraces in the midst of luxuriant virgin forest.

'Fastastic,' I said, 'and what about Soto?'

'If it suits you, you can meet him at the University at eleven o'clock tomorrow morning.'

It is easy to find one's way about in the big city. Bogotá is covered by a network of streets intersecting at right angles. All the streets running from north to south are called *carreras*, except for occasional grandiose *avenidas*. The streets which cross the *carreras* at right angles are called *calles* and like the larger streets running from north to south they are numbered consecutively.

I arrived punctually at eleven o'clock at Professor Soto's Institute on Carrera No. 1. The tall slim archaeologist greeted me with a smile.

'So you're the man who writes those books!'

'Do you think I shouldn't?' I countered.

'Not at all. Science is open to all opinions.'

So the professor, quite young to hold a chair at the age of 38, was prepared to accept views outside the standard dogmas. I admired him as a rare example of his profession.

In an auditorium we sat in chairs with an arm rest on the right so that the students could take notes. The professor lolled on the seat and puffed at a cigarette. I asked: 'You call the lost city Buritaca 200. What does that mean?'

'The Sierra Nevada of Santa Marta extends between 32° 50′

Professor Alvaro Soto Holguin received me at his institute in the university for our first conversation.

and 74° 15′ west of Greenwich. Latitudinally the region comprises latitudes of 10° 5′ and 11° 20′ situated north of the Equator. Several small rivers have their sources in this region and some of them flow into the Caribbean in north-westerly direction. One of them is the Rio Buritaca, on the banks of which the "Lost City" is located. Hence Buritaca 200.'

'But what does the number 200 mean?'

'It is the two hundredth settlement, the two hundredth city, so to speak, that we have located so far.'

'It sound incredible. Does that mean that the whole jungle area was once dotted with settlements and urban cultures?'

'Yes, the area is enormous. You can form a rough idea of it when I tell you that we already know more than 2,000 kilometres of roads and tracks with stone surfaces. We have been excavating since 1976 and there is no end in sight. Buritaca 200 alone is ten times as big as the famous Inca fortress of Macchu Picchu in Peru.'

A girl student served us coffee. Colombian coffee tastes good all over the world, but it is never made so strong as in its home country. It would be interesting to know whether the Colombians all have heart disease or whether they hardly know where their hearts are beating because of the coffee. I asked; 'When was the city built and by whom?'

'On the basis of previous datings using the radioactive carbon isotope carbon 14, we conclude that Buritaca 200 was built around AD 800. The builders were the Tairona Indians, a sub-group of the Chibcha. Scholars also speak of a Tairona culture, but that is absurd, because the Tairona did not use that name for themselves. It was the Spaniards who gave the name to the Indians living in the Sierra Nevada. Not such a strange name when you know that the word *tairo* means something like 'casting metal' and the gold-hungry conquerors were only out after metal.'

'Did you find pottery or graves with mummies in?'

'We found ceramics and some metal objects. We discovered a few rockfaces with engravings and even some graves, but without mummies. The jungle is too humid for mummification.'

'Is it true that the excavation area is sealed off by the army?'

'Sealed off? That's not the right word. There are a few

soldiers up there to protect our personnel and keep out grave-robbers who could do a lot of damage.'

'So you have nothing to hide on the site? Theoretically, could tourists visit Buritaca 200 on organised tours?'

'We have nothing to hide, but we do not want tourists on the site. We are quite willing to allow access to experts, who could learn a lot from Buritaca 200. The social and ecological system of the complex is imposing. Although the Indian builders practised agriculture, traded with the sea ports and built cities, they did not destroy their environment.'

'Have you any objection to my visiting Buritaca 200?'

'Not the slightest!'

'How can I get there?'

'Only by helicopter. The flight from Bogotá to Santa Marta and back costs about 8,000 US dollars. But if you have the time and can wait for two months, because I have to give my university lectures, you can fly with me.'

A kind offer, but how to spend two months, a sixth of a year? I told myself that I must not be downhearted.

My first conversation with Soto Holguin was comparatively short, but later we had two lengthy talks at his flat in a high-rise building on Calle No. 7. Gradually I began to form a picture of the Lost City, as parts of the jigsaw fitted together. This is its story.

When the Spaniards Rodrigo de Bastidas and Juan de la Cosa were investigating the coasts of Venezuela in 1501, they also went in the direction of Panama. Obviously they must have traded with the Indians in the coastal regions, for they left one of their companions, Juan de Buenaventura, to learn the Indians' language. After all, merchants have to learn the language of their trading partners before they can cheat them.

The conquerors soon realised that Indians had gold objects to barter, as well as other things.

Professor Henning Bischof (2), the foremost expert on the Tairona culture, writes of the dense settlement in the region of the present-day port of Santa Marta:

In the sixteenth and early seventeenth centuries the Sierra Nevada looked quite different ... This conclusion is confirmed by the accounts of expeditions and battles, which show that the Spaniards had a much better range of vision than would have been the case in wooded mountain country. Basically, details of the density of the Indian population alone are enough to prove that the landscape must have changed considerably.

Rodrigo de Bastidas settled in Santo Domingo, the present-day capital of the Dominican Republic on the south coast of Haiti. In 1514 the Spanish king Carlos I appointed him Governor of the recently founded Province of Santa Marta. The Governor reached the small coastal town of Santa Marta with a body of two or three hundred men in June 1526.

During the next few decades the Spaniards were in almost continuous combat with the Tairona Indians, who defended themselves desperately against the white invaders who burnt their villages, plundered them and took the men prisoner or slaughtered them. The *conquistadores* knew that their barbaric methods had the blessing of the king in Madrid. He had issued a decree turning the Indians into slaves, outlawing them and allowing them to be killed or forced to perform the most degrading tasks.

The Indians met the Spaniards' modern weapons with stones, wooden clubs, spears and bows and arrows. Poisoned arrows. They got the poison from two natural sources, firstly the juice of the manzanilla tree, a highly poisonous type of spurge with fruit-like apples, which contained the poison. The arrows were dipped into the juice, dried in the air and wrapped in palm leaves so that the archers themselves would not be poisoned. Secondly, they tapped pacurine from the bark of the liana *Strychnos Toxifera*. In modern medicine it is known as curare, used as a nerve-relaxant. The Indians liked using pacurine because the game they killed remained edible in spite of the poison once the edges round the wound were cut out carefully.

Thousands of Spaniards died painfully by poisoned arrows in a hundred years' war against the Tairona, but the number of Indians who paid with their lives was far greater; it is estimated at 10,000.

Repelled by all the brutality, Juan de Castellanos (3), an eyewitness used to horrors, told how Captain Miguel Pinol gave orders that all Indians taken prisoner should have 'their noses, ears and lips cut off'. More then 70 Indian leaders were massacred, as well as women and children, and a severely wounded prince's son was executed, but not until the pagan son had been baptised into the Roman Catholic Church.

When it was all over the Spaniards had looted several hundred thousand gold pesos, as well as jewels and pearls. Indian settlements in the Sierra Nevada were destroyed. The few surviving Tairona hid in remote bays on the Caribbean coast.

The Tairona culture was wiped out and forgotten. Centuries passed. The jungle swallowed up the once flowering fields and settlements and cities. Save that in the region around Santa Marta it was rumoured that somewhere in the steaming forest-clad mountains there had once been an Indian tribe who saved a lot of gold from the Spaniards.

The kingdom of the Tairona had long since become the habitat of wild cats, apes, eagles and poisonous snakes. The humid flora of the primeval forest had conquered it. But gold has an irresistible fascination and men with gold-fever are not afraid of anything.

In autumn 1940 the treasure hunter and amateur archaeologist Florentino Sepúlveda met an old member of the Kogi Indian tribe in a quiet bay on the caribbean, only 20 km from Santa Marta. The old man told him that there were great cities and endless roads that had once been built by the Tairona in the immediate vicinity.

Sepúlveda, who was sixty years old himself, did not take the Indian's tales at their face value, but he found them interesting enough to tell his 19-year-old son Julio Cesar about them.

Julio Cesar, who did not know much more about the Spanish conquerors than that they loved gold, took the story seriously. For he was convinced of the existence of the legendary land of El Dorado and sensed that here was a chance to get rich quick — like winning the pools.

Julio Cesar followed the river Buritaca upstream from the coast. In the spring of 1975 he stumbled on one of the terraces of the Lost City. Convinced that he was on the right track, he took a spade and hacked a hole in the wall in front of him. After hours of laborious work he had to admit that the wall he was banging away at was part of a huge flight of steps.

This brought the gold-digger to his senses. He got on his horse and rode back to the port and seaside resort of Santa Marta, a difficult seven days' ride.

In a hotel bar, Julio Cesar did what a grave-robber should never do. He talked. Greedy for the gold, but not able to solve the problem of the site on his own, he showed the place in the jungle to some companions. Either out of envy or gold-fever, someone later shot Julio Cesar in the Lost City. Comrades dug his grave near the steps on which he had stumbled.

Then the grave-robbers, the *guaqueros*, swarmed in. They found their way into overgrown stone ruins. Soon Tairona cult artefacts appeared more and more frequently on the black market in antiques. The Colombian Institute for Anthropology and Archaeology got wind of this. When one grave-robber ransacked the site, the army took over the Lost City.

Archaeologists have been excavating in the jungle of the Sierra Nevada since 1976 and there is no end in sight yet, as Professor Soto told me. According to an assessment of the complexes so far excavated, 300,000 Indians must have lived there once. That is equal to the combined populations of Geneva and Berne.

Who were these wild Tairona Indians who managed to build these gigantic cities, who could not defend themselves against a handful of Spanish conquerors?

Soto told me that the present-day Kogi Indians on the coast and in the valleys of the Sierra Nevada are most probably direct descendants of the Tairona. His teacher, Professor Gerardo Reichel-Dolmatoff, spent years studying the life and history of the Kogi. In the process he established so many astonishing similarities between the present-day Kogi and the more ancient Tairona that we can assume that the Kogi descended from the Tairona.

Therefore groups of Tairona must have survived the Spanish massacres, preserved their ancient traditions and religious customs and handed them down to later generations. To find out who the Tairona were, I would have to concentrate on the Kogi, who are still living.

Once again Professor Preuss was the first man to take a scholarly interest in the Kogi and describe them in detail. After he had excavated parts of San Agustín from 1913 to

1914, he tackled the traditions of the Kágaba, as the Kogi were formerly called. Preuss discovered that the Kágaba-Kogi attributed the creation to the primordial mother Gauteóvan, who produced the sun and everything that existed from her menstrual blood. The four original priests who were the ancestors of the present-day Kogi priestly tribe also stemmed from Gauteóvan.

Tradition had it that the four original priests brought culture to the Indians, made laws and instructed them 'in all things'. The original priests had their home in space. Laws reached the Kágaba 'from outside'. It was said that these priests wore masks when they arrived and had their 'faces taken away'. If we assume that they had arrived on an interstellar flight, the faces would have been oxygen masks.

The priests bequeathed their office to their sons. They were brought up in the temple, serving a nine-year novitiate, so that the knowledge of the fathers was handed down untouched from one generation to another. The highest priests of the Kágaba-Kogi are called *Mama* (5). The *Mama* are more than what we normally understand by priests. The *Mama* is the absolute ruler of the tribe, whose orders must be followed blindly. There is no limit to the praise and punishment he can allot, because he knows that he is in direct succession to the original cosmic priests. Even today the *Mama* is convinced that he is in spiritual communication with the cosmos.

In order to reach this high-priestly rank, novices were shut up for nine years in total darkness and under close supervision in order to develop hypersensitive spirituality for cosmic contacts. The poor lads could not touch a woman during these nine years, do any work or eat salt. They were not served with food until midnight. It consisted of haricot beans, potatoes and snails; nothing with blood in it.

The primordial mother Gauteóvan and the four priests were not the only ones to emerge from the universe. There was also Uncle Nivaleue, who descended from heaven and made himself useful by laying out large fields. The demon Namsaui was another heavenly figure. The myths say that he was twice the size of normal men and killed men by the cold which flowed from him, leaving only their bones behind (4). It was said of Namsaui that his mask was red, his clothing blue and that he had protruding eyes over a very long nose. Namsaui was the

lightning demon; he made the thunder and the snow that falls
from heaven.

Professor Preuss described the Kágaba creation myth over
50 years ago. From the 30 pages he wrote I extract only the
most important verses which show that their gods came from
space and made man intelligent.

1st verse: The mother of our whole tribe bore us in the
            beginning. She is the mother of all kinds of
            men and she is the mother of all tribes ...

2nd verse: She alone is the mother of fire, the mother of
            the sun and the Milky Way ...

12th verse: And thus did the mother leave a memorial in
            every temple. Together with her sons Sintana,
            Seizankuan, Aluanuiko and Kultsavitabauya,
            she left behind songs and dances as memori-
            als.

13th verse: That is what the priests, fathers and elder
            brothers reported.

Then come tales of the four priests fighting with demons
and animals. 'Lightning bolts' are unleashed; there were flights
all over the heavens and seeds of various plants were brought
to earth. Masks of the gods were worn, one of them hidden
in a mountain:

30th verse: Today it was set up to work on diseases and
            all kinds of evil and so that the novices who
            had learnt in the temple could talk to it. After-
            wards the fathers, priests and elder brothers
            talked to it.

Did I read aright? Priests in ancient times are supposed to
have talked to a mask to influence diseases? These descriptions
only become intelligible when looked at from a modern point
of view. The mask was a helmet with a built-in radio connection via which the priests received expert advice.

Knowledge of the Flood shows how far back the mythology
of the Kágaba-Kogi reaches:

38th verse: Now centuries passed and then this world
            produced men with unnatural tendencies so
            that they used all kinds of animals to couple
            with. The mother desired the son, the father
            the daughter, the brother the sister, all being
            of the same blood.

39th verse: The prince Zantana saw this and opened the gates of heaven so that it rained for four years.

40th verse: When the priests observed that he would do this, the priest Seizankua built a magic ship and put all kinds of animals and other things inside it: the four-footed animals, the birds, and all kinds of plants did he place inside it. Thereupon the elder brother Mulkueikai entered the magic ship and closed the door.

41st verse: Then began red and blue rain which lasted for four years, and with the rain seas spread all over the world.

42nd verse: Meanwhile elder brother Mulkueikai lay in the magic ship which afterwards settled on the crest of the Sierra Negra. There he ventured out briefly and only very close to the ship. He stayed on the Sierra Negra for nine days.

43rd verse: After those nine days nine centuries passed before all the seas dried out, as the priests have handed down in our traditions.

44th verse: Now all evil people had perished, *and the priests, the elder brothers, all came down from heaven*. Whereupon Mulkueikai opened the door and placed all the birds and four-footed animals, all the trees and plants here on the earth. This did the divine person called father Kalgusiza bring about.

46th verse: And in all the temples they left behind a souvenir as a memorial.

How closely the texts resemble each other!

The Kágaba tradition mentioned sodomy, as did Moses in Genesis 19, before the destruction of Sodom and Gomorrah. The Sumerian *Epic of Gilgamesh* also includes a similar account of the Flood.

The Kágaba myth says that the priests all came down from heaven. The Sumerian King List says that: 'After the flood had receded, the kingdom came down from heaven again.' It sounds just like the Epic of Gilgamesh which relates that the 'gods' came down to earth after the great Flood.

Is there anyone barefaced enough to talk about coincidences when faced with such striking similarities? I mention only two myths identical with the Kágaba creation story, but they are found in ancient traditions all over the world. Everywhere real life experiences find their way into the myths.

Generations of priests continuously handed down the ancient knowledge of their cosmic teachers and preserved it. Professor Reichel-Dolmatoff (6) has shown that all the activities of the Kogi are still permeated by the cosmic laws of their Kágaba ancestors.

The Kogi are deeply religious. Their religious ideas are closely connected with their conception of order and happenings in the universe. Most villages have a chief who embodies governmental authority, but the real power of decision lies in the hands of the *Mama*, the native priests. These men have a thorough knowledge of tribal customs. They are not only shamans or medicine-men, but also in their priestly role take on tasks which they perform during ceremonial rituals after years of training.

During his years of study, Reichel-Dolmatoff discovered that all Kogi buildings could only by understood in the context of cosmic processes.

If a terrace, a house or a temple was to be built, the primary concerns were not only about the presence of water, light and shade, but the Kogi's cosmic relations to the constellations and the calendar were also 'built in'.

The Kogi looked on the cosmos as egg-shaped, demarcated by seven points: north, south, west, east, zenith, nadir (the lowest point of the heavens diametrically opposite to the zenith) and the centre. Within the space defined in this way lie nine layers, nine worlds, the middle or fifth layer representing our world. All the temples and ceremonial houses are models of the Kogi cosmos and follow this pattern.

Inside the ceremonial houses four divisions are superimposed. On the fifth division, the earth, the Kogi live, but symbolically four more divisions lead down into the earth, as symbol of the cosmos.

Apart from being religious centres, Kogi temples are also observatories. They are laid out in such a way that an accurate

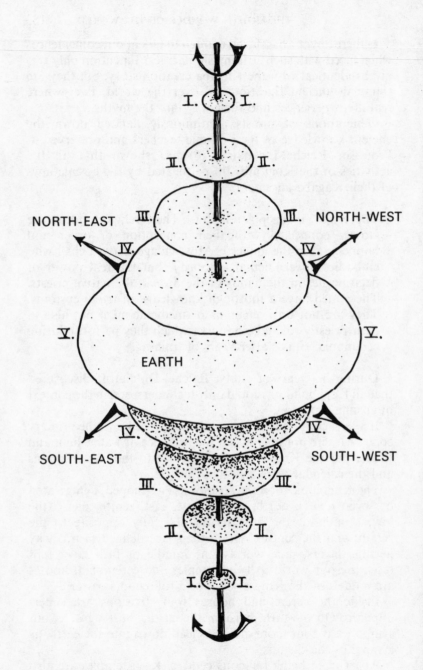

The Kogi looked on the cosmos as egg-shaped space.

calendar reading is possible at any time. Reichel-Dolmatoff (7) gives this example:

Men and women live apart. In every Kogi village there is a large round men's house on the roof of which a big post like a flagpole points up to heaven. Directly opposite — after all, the ladies must not be too far away — is the women's house, which is round, too. Two crossed beams emerge from the roof-ridge. Post and beams represent a symbolical act!

Precisely on 21 March, the beginning of spring, the post on the roof of the men's house throws a long shadow on the ground. It falls exactly between the shadows cast by the crossed beams on the women's house. The phallus penetrates the vagina, a symbol of spring. Seeds must be laid in the earth.

Inside the temple, a thick rope hangs from the ridge post through the four divisions down to the fifth, the earth. The high priest Mama is convinced that he is in direct contact with his cosmic teachers through this rope.

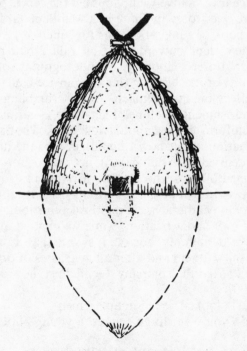

Cross-section of a Kogi house with its symbolic continuation into the ground.

What does this tell us? Nine years' confinement in the dark might develop telepathic abilities enabling men to make contact with extraterrestrials. We know that radio connections from star to star are too slow to make interstellar communication possible. Alpha Centauri, the nearest fixed star to the earth, is four light-years away, i.e. 4 times 9.46 times 10^{12} km. Questions from earth transmitted to Alpha Centauri by radio would not get a radio answer for eight years. But telepathy is as swift as thought and it is not bound by the physical laws of time and space. Could the Kogi's knowledge make the inaccessible intelligible to us?

When I had given my lectures in the Teatro Libertador and used up the time allotted for talking to Professor Soto and visits to libraries, I was burning to see the Lost City about whose builders I now knew quite a lot.

Salvation came from an angle indicated three months before, and then by a lucky chance.

I was invited as a guest to the Officers' Club of the FAC.* The air force owns a lovely clubhouse in the centre of Bogotá, an extensive one-storey building in a well-kept garden with a swimming pool. My invitation was for lunch.

From one o'clock onwards I sat on a dark-blue plush sofa next to Dr Forero, looking at photographs of famous Colombian aviators. Neither this nor an ice-cold vermouth had any effect on my stomach. It was rumbling irritably, craving nourishment. Colonel Baer-Ruiz, wearing a smart light-blue uniform, arrived about two o'clock. The first reasonable information about how I could get into the jungle near Santa Marta dried up in polite introductions to group captains and pensioned officers who kept on arriving in droves.

When we sat down at the beautifully set-out table around three o'clock, my stomach, as loud as a ventriloquist's voice, interrupted every conversation, while we chatted about God and the world and my books. I swore that I would get something out of them and after a few glasses of dry Chilean white wine I asked the company 'Gentlemen, how do I get to Buritaca 200?'

The officers looked at me in amazement.

'Where do you want to go?' asked a young pilot.

* *Fuerza Aerea Colombiana*, the Colombian Air Force.

The forest flora have forced their way through the man-made paving stones.

'The whole site has a plan, a gigantic plan...'

Above:
A last snapshot: Sylvia, Margarita, Hernando and the flight engineer, shortly before takeoff.

Overleaf
Left:
Millions of cubic metres of stone were shifted at Buritaca. How? The eighth wonder of the world?

Right:
We hastened up the main flight of steps to the landing terrace. The helicopter took off and the landing place was swallowed up in the maws of the greedy rain forest.

I soon realised that Buritaca 200 was so much double-Dutch to these aviators. Admittedly they had heard of the Lost City, but no one had even a rough idea where it was. Well briefed by Professor Soto, the little Swiss gentleman was able to give the astonished Colombians the exact geographical location of their national attraction.

I asked politely if there was any chance of looking for it in a helicopter. All the officers burst into a cascade of Spanish which I could no longer follow. Finally Colonel Baer told me that only the head of the air force, General Paredes Diago, could decide about my case. However he had just returned from a ten-day visit to the USA and his timetable was so booked up that he would not be able to receive me at once. *Mañana*.

'What a pity,' I said and saw my prey escaping. How was I to get into the jungle, unless I waited for two months and relied on Professor Soto?

Over coffee and brandy, I overheard someone saying that General Paredes Diago was interested in my books and was also a passionate pipe collector.

The pipe which opened up the jungle to me.

Pipe collector? An idea flashed through my brain.

Since I got hold of a patented model which makes tiresome cleaning with dirty fingers unnecessary, I smoke a pipe for lazy smokers while working or playing chess. This pipe does not have the classical curved bowl. A container closed by a filter holds the tobacco and is in a straight line with the mouthpiece. The container can easily be emptied into an ashtray by a slight pressure. I took a brand-new example out of my jacket pocket. 'Does the general know this sort of pipe?'

Colonel Baer was interested at once. I took the pipe to bits, put it together again and asked him to present it to the general with my compliments and possibly mention that he was the only man in Colombia who could help to solve my little problem.

Colonel Baer-Ruiz phoned me early the next morning to say that General Paredes Diago would expect me in the headquarters of the FAC at 4 p.m. Dr Forero also accompanied me on this vital visit.

The air force headquarters, a modern building of glass, steel and concrete, lies on the outskirts of Bogotá. My hand luggage was checked and our bodies were searched. After showing our own identity cards, a corporal pinned numbered cards to our chests, the only military identification I have ever worn.

On the way to the general's office past glass cases full of model aircraft of all periods, we civilians were given appraising looks by officers who were waiting for their appointments on leather settees. We only sat in the waiting room for a quarter of an hour and the door to the holy of holies opened.

General Paredes Diago, with five gold stars on his shoulder straps, held my pipe in his hand when he rose from behind his desk. He asked us to sit down in a corner while an orderly served coffee. My poor heart!

I gave the general a signed copy of the Spanish version of my book *Signs of the Gods?*, *Profeta del Pasado*. Warned in advance that the general was a busy man, I came straight to the point: I wanted a helicopter flight to Buritaca 200.

For a moment the general looked at me reflectively. Then he summoned his adjutant.

'What unit is stationed in Santa Marta?'

'The No. 5 Cordova Infantry Battalion, sir,' answered the young officer.

'Find out at once whether the battalion has a helicopter and whether the machine is ready for a special mission the day after tomorrow.'

A loudspeaker somewhere interrupted our conversation. The general spoke something in reply into his microphone. I could not understand a word. The general bowed to me and disappeared. Dr Forero gave the thumbs-up sign. We had won!

In a few minutes the general returned, handed me an envelope and wished me luck and success.

In the taxi I read what the general had dictated:

Fuerza Aerea Colombiana.
Senor Teniente Coronel.
Hector Lopez Ramirez Commandante Batallón de Infanteria No. 5 Cordova Santa Marta.
El señor Erich von Däniken está autorizado por este Comando para efectuar un vuelo en Helicótero Hughes que se encuentra en esa Unidad de la ciudad de Santa Marta a la ciudad perdida.
Cordial saludo.
General Raul Alberto Paredes Diago.
Commandante Fuerza Aérea.

[Lt Colonel Hector Lopez Ramirez
Officer commanding No. 5 Cordova Infantry Battalion Santa Marta
This order authorises Mr Erich von Däniken to fly from Santa Marta to the Lost City in the Hughes Helicopter belonging to your unit.]

The next day I landed in Santa Marta on the noon flight of Colombian Airways and lodged right by the sea in the Irotama, a hotel which had seen better days. I phoned repeatedly but I could not get in touch with Colonel Ramirez. At five o'clock in the afternoon it's packing-up time, as with soldiers all over the world. *Mañana.*

On Friday, 21 August, at 5.30 a.m., I was driven out to No. 5 Infantry Battalion. Two infantrymen with machine pistols searched me at the entrance before I could explain the reason for my visit, but the general's letter which I waved at them worked like an open sesame until a civilian in the colonel's anteroom looked at it with wrinkled brows. Surprise departures from routine were unwelcome at such an early hour. The civilian disappeared into the next door office without a word.

Although it was so early in the morning I was dripping with sweat because of the high humidity. I sat on a wooden bench, wiping the sweat from my forehead with a handkerchief that was already wet, and waited. The civilian returned, sat at his desk and said nothing. The waiting seemed endless. Was there going to be some snag when I was almost there?

I determined to sit there quietly, but determined not to budge until the general's order was carried out. *Basta.*

Basta!, repeated the young man in green uniform who was leaning against the wall with his arms crossed. On the flap of his right-hand breast pocket I saw the words Fuerza Aerea Colombiana embroidered in silver. A pilot in the infantry?

He had to be my helicopter pilot! I spoke to him.

His name was Fernando, he said, and he was to fly a Mr von Däniken to the Lost City, but he had not the faintest idea where it was and the weather that day was not ideally suited to the little Hughes. Besides the machine could only stay airborne for two and a half hours. It could not spend much time searching because if the city could not be found in an hour and a quarter we should have to return.

Fernando did not see things through rose-coloured spectacles. He gave a gloomy account of the difficulties he had with the marijuana cultivators in the district. They were rightly afraid of the military pilots and opened fire on them at random. More than one aircraft had been shot down over the forests and the crew had never been heard of again. Santa Marta was a centre of the trade in marijuana, a city where life was not worth twopence since, trafficking in the drug had begun. People could earn fantastic sums in a very short time and that pushed up inflation. Morality went to pot and shoot-outs were the order of the day. 'Santa Marta gold' was dealt with on the international markets at top prices as being finest quality marijuana.

Since the men stood to attention, the officer who looked in and held the door open must be my Colonel Ramirez. I leapt up, gave my name, received a brief searching look and was invited to sit down in his office. Naturally we were served coffee, of the kind that pours forth from morning to night.

Santa Marta — port and seaside resort on the Caribbean — is the centre of traffic in illegal 'Santa Marta gold', valuable marijuana.

Fernando described his difficulties. Colonel Ramirez interrupted him. 'Is there anyone in the battalion who knows the exact location of the Lost City?'

Ramirez gave an order over the loudspeaker, spread some military maps on the table and pointed with his finger. 'It's somewhere in that region.'

When I pointed out that it was on the River Buritaca, Fernando asked ironically if I knew the forest. He could not land there. I would either have to jump out or be let down on a rope ladder. I certainly had no desire to do that and said firmly, 'You can land in the forest on terraces that were built more than a thousand years ago!'

Professor Soto had told me that that was how he had reached the site.

'Do you believe that?' Colonel Ramirez looked at me sceptically.

'I know it for a fact.'

A corporal, who was undoubtedly of Indian blood, reported.

'You've been to the Lost City before?' asked Ramirez.

'Yes, Señor Comandante,' said the Indian, thumping his chest proudly.

'Then you shall go on the flight.'

Until that moment I did not realise that even Indians can turn white. The corporal crossed himself and his face, which had been radiant, turned ashen.

Together with Hernando, the Indian and a flight engineer, I clambered into the four-seater helicopter, which crossed Santa Marta with a deafening roar, then flew along the coast to the mouth of the Buritaca valley.

The natives were called Indians (Indios) by mistake. To the end of his days Columbus believed that the country he discovered was India and so named the inhabitants Indians. The Indian shouted something I did not understand and I saw that he was showing Hernando where to fly in sign language. Low cloud cover clung to the tops of the giant forest trees. Somewhere down below there were marijuana farmers, but I was more afraid of losing our way than their flintlocks. There was nothing to orientate oneself by. From above the green hell looked like an enormous greenish-black cauliflower. Dense and impenetrable.

The helicopter banked steeply and then I saw it: one terrace with a second and a third one below it Hernando had spotted it, too, and gave me a significant look. He landed the Hughes gently on the topmost terrace. He did not stop the rotor blades. They made a whirlwind in the still air. Hernando was anxious to take off again; he did not trust the weather.

'Back here in five hours,' I shouted and put up my hand with the fingers outspread. 'OK. In five hours,' he shouted back, pointing to the terrace on which we stood.

The helicopter rose up vertically; its clatter seemed to cling to trees and lianas. When the noise had faded, there was a moment's silence in the jungle, but the animals soon recovered from their fear of the noisy visit. Monkeys roared, birds chattered and invisible animals screamed. Wherever I went I was followed by buzzing mosquitoes which proved to be very attentive. I would gladly have walked around the jungle sauna

When the helicopter banked we saw a terrace suitable for landing in the dense jungle.

like Adam, but the repulsive biters made me realise in the most unpleasant way that I was not in Paradise. I read somewhere that there were about 1.5 million species of insects. The great majority of them were represented in Buritaca.

Now I was standing lost in the Lost city, probably the first European to do so. Certainly no European had as yet photographed or written about the site.

I like adventure, but I'm no hero. I am always getting into tricky situations against my will. I asked myself what would happen if the weather made landing impossible in five hours. Or supposing the only helicopter available crashed in the meantime.

What if Hernando was given a more important military mission? Spending the night here was not a very pleasant prospect, but what could I do about it? I shouldered my cameras and clambered down to the next terrace.

Opposite, on the cliff face, clung a wooden hut among tropical undergrowth, cedars, nut trees, eucalyptus trees, advocado pear trees, rubber trees, palms and ferns, all of them smothered in lianas. It had to be the archaeologists' camp. I shouted, but there was no answer. Heaven only knew where the team were digging today to keep the greedy jungle at bay from the ruins they had excavated. They must have seen and heard the helicopter.

Suddenly two soldiers appeared from nowhere. They were wearing jungle camouflage suits flecked with brown, green and red and were armed with rifles and pistols.

'*Buenos días, señores!*' I cried but got no reaction from their dark-brown faces. I still had two duty-free cigars in metal tubes bought on the Lufthansa flight and I gave them to the soldiers. They said, '*Gracias!*' and walked away. They were far from loquacious, but at least I knew that there were people somewhere in the green hothouse.

I slowly descended the endless steps which were a good 1.5 m wide and was surprised that the elliptical terrace on which we had landed was still within my field of vision. The lower I went, the more obvious it became that the topmost platform rested on a lower one, and that on another one and so on. A series of artificial stone plateaux carried the structure up to the summit.

Was I suffering from hallucinations? I met two delightful girls on a moss-covered path. One of them, wearing baggy trousers and a green safari blouse, smiled and shook me by the hand. 'My name is Sylvia. Welcome to Buritaca 200!'

The other Amazon, in blue jeans that showed off her appetising figure, a wide leather belt and a wide-brimmed straw hat, looked a little bit older than Sylvia. Margarita, the older girl, was an architect by profession; Sylvia, an archaeologist, had been working with the excavation team for more than half a year.

My Colombian forest angels asked me for a cigarette, the only thing they longed for at that moment. I gave them all I had left. These girls with their perfect English were just what I needed. They led me along stone paths through the tropical rain forest, commenting on the site as we went. The humidity remained steady, between 60 and 95 per cent.

Buritaca 200 lies to right and left of the little river that gave the town its name, clinging to the gorges of Cerro Corea, 3,055 m high. The structures are arranged in the form of terraces in several layers along a broad road. The main entrance to the town is 900 m high. From the end of a gorge, a steep flight of steps with a gradient of 50 degrees leads 1,100 m up to the large levelled terraces. The upper part seems to have been the centre of the city. An intricate mixture of 26 large and small terraces with areas varying between 50 and 880 sq. m occupy the heights. All these terraces have been excavated since 1976, a tremendous feat.

Complicated topographical conditions were laid down by nature. This means that the ancient architects had to level the mountain metre by metre to make room for the horizontal structures. They cut into the rock faces, filling in with stones, earth and supporting walls. The height of the wall varies from 60 cm to 10 m!

Integrated with walls and terraces, the excavators discovered a canalisation system which kept the vast complex dry in spite of the constant humidity and torrential rain.

Margarita explained to me that archaeologists divided Buritaca into four main sectors. In the first sector they found the remains of household objects such as stone mills for grinding corn, in the second pottery, such as scoops, vases and eating dishes, in the third, ceremonial artefacts including beautifully worked clay flutes, and in the fourth, cult objects such as priests' rings, figurines of the gods and funerary tributes.

In spite of these finds, archaeologists, especially Soto Holguin, the Director of Excavations, are faced with a problem. No one knows what Buritaca really was — a sanctuary on a vast scale, orientated to the firmament, the calendar? A priestly city inhabited solely by initiates in one vast monastery? A dormitory town in which 300,000 Indians slept before going to work somewhere else in the daytime? Was it a military outpost, a fortress?

However, scholars do agree that the builders of the jungle city included far-sighted architects and engineers with a variety of skills. The whole conception implies far-sightedness because the settlements in the Sierra Nevada cannot have been the work of one generation. The gigantic scale shows that there must have been an overall plan before the first great stones were moved. Astronomers must have been involved from the beginning, at least as advisers, as it has been proved that certain terraces are aligned on the constellations. The exemplary ecological system indicates the cooperation of engineers. There were only limited areas for cultivation, but maize, beans, manioc and potatoes to supply 300,000 Indians were cultivated without destroying the environment.

In order to understand the full significance of this achievement, one needs to know the state of affairs around Santa Marta before 1975, when the Sierra Nevada was placed under government protection. The population in the port, the smart seaside resort of Santa Marta, grew at an alarming rate. It overflowed the city limits and reached the slopes of the Sierra Nevada. The forest was burnt down. People planted coffee and bananas in the fertile soil for a couple of years and as yields decreased pushed further into the jungle, leaving behind the scars of civilisation. In this district, it rains virtually every day from April to November. Without the protective covering of the tropical trees and their network of roots in the ground, the soil is eroded. The land becomes arid and unfertile in a

The Tairona settled in the virgin forest, but they did not destroy it.

few years. Today the area around Santa Marta still bears tragic witness to the destructive type of agriculture practised by local settlers until 1975. A disaster.

All this happened in a relatively short time. Yet the Tairona lived in their cities for nearly a thousand years without destroying the virgin forest and still produced great quantities of agricultural products. How did the Tairona solve their ecological and agricultural problems? Professor Soto gave me this answer:

To achieve what was achieved at Buritaca there must have been a social organisation that differed from every other type. The Tairona Indians must have known and used something special. These people were anything but primitive and the modern world can only learn from them. We destroy tropical rain forests by slash and burn and keep on creating new environmental crises. The builders of these settlements proved that there are other ways of going about things.

At first I suspected that the topmost terrace had come about by a chance accumulation of stone slabs and blocks.

At first I suspected that the top terrace had been formed by a chance accumulation of stone slabs. I said as much to Sylvia and Margarita, but they pointed out that I was standing in a landscape intentionally laid out in a bizarre way, a landscape of stone circles, walls, ellipses, small towers, flights of steps and paths, in an indescribable confusion of shapes which would not have occurred to Pablo Picasso in his most daring period, when he was dissolving the objective into geometrical structures.

Sylvia pulled curtains of lianas aside and opened up a vista of new surprises which extended downhill to the River Buritaca and up to the rock faces. Wherever we went in this ill-understood monument to the past, we continuously came across artificially levelled surfaces. The Hanging Gardens of Semiramis in Babylon were looked on as the seventh wonder of the world. I make a plea for adding Buritaca as the eighth wonder of the world.

The girls watched me as I came on one surprise after another. My camera was clicking away constantly. If I could not prove

My camera never stopped clicking!

what I saw with photographs, no one would believe my description of the unique panorama. I had only to push aside the enormous leaf of a rubber tree to find myself staring at yet more massive accurately built walls and paths. With the explosive power of forest flora, thick corozo palms, bay-trees, cedars and ferns of every kind had forced their way through the neatly laid stones. It was a labyrinth as described in the dictionary: an arrangement of tortuous and deceptive paths from which it is difficult to find the way out. No matter whether I looked up, down, right or left, more platforms lay around me.

Mentally I conjured up the distant past when the priests worshipped their gods on the highest terraces, surrounded by thousands of Indians. When incense offerings rose to heaven from every platform and combined with the prayers, when the *Mama* were on intimate terms with the cosmos. If you block out in your imagination the trees which grow on the slopes today, a complete picture of this utopian landscape is present. Professor Soto's remark came into mind: 'The whole site has a plan, a gigantic plan, save that we do not know what it was for!'

One stone, more than two metres high, was covered with a plastic sack. I asked what it was. Sylvia and Margarita undid the rope and removed the protective covering from the monster, which was a monolith with many right-angled lines engraved on it. 'What is it?' I repeated.

Sylvia answered. 'The Indians say it was the plan of the complex.'

'A sort of city map, in other words?'

The girl nodded, but added at once that Professor Soto had his doubts about that. He had had the stone covered to save it from further weathering, in the hope that one day it would yield up its secret to scholars.

The literally indescribable noises of the forest were suddenly overpowered by the sound of water, although water was nowhere to be seen. Sylvia and Margarita were amused by my astonishment, then they pulled aside a curtain of lianas. A waterfall poured down the cliff until it was captured in a broad stone channel and led by another channel to a circular platform.

When you think that this area with its tropic rain was kept dry, your respect for the constructors increases enormously.

The Indians claim that this stone shows the town plan of Buritaca. It is not yet known if that is true.

I know the famous rice terraces in the mountains of the Philippines and the steep cultivated terraces of Machu Picchu in Peru. None of them is comparable with Buritaca 200.

The builders here did not set to work with monoliths of monstrous dimensions, as at Tiahuanaco and Puma Punku in Bolivia, or like Sacsayhuaman in Peru, and yet millions of cubic metres of stone were moved, for all the mountain slopes turn out to be artificially built on. After the first finds, the incredible astonishment began that always sets in in the presence of new discoveries. We shall keep on learning new things about Buritaca 200.

Suddenly monkeys and birds were silent. The noise of the helicopter's rotors echoed from the slopes. My five hours had actually passed.

Sylvia, Margarita and I hastened along narrow paths and across the main flight of steps to the landing terrace. Without the girls topographical knowledge, I would have been hopelessly lost.

Hernando was chatting to the soldiers who had been so taciturn with me. I pulled out of my pockets everything I did not need urgently and gave the conents to the helpful ladies: a light NASA windcheater, an anti-insect spray, plasters for cuts, a dynamo pocket torch, two screwdrivers and a measuring tape. Everything can be put to some use in the jungle.

The helicopter took off and flew low over the treetops in a curve back to the sea. Our landing place was left behind and was swallowed up by the mouth of the greedy rain forest.

Professor Soto had told me that the Kogi, like their ancestors the Tairona, looked on themselves as the 'elder brothers' of our planet. All foreigners are 'younger brothers' to them, for it was their ancient priests who brought life to their country from the cosmos.

The Tairona once had a blooming culture. Why do the Kogi dress so wretchedly today? Why have they stopped working in gold, spinning thread and weaving artistic materials? Why do they no longer paint mythical scenes on their ceramics?

The *Mama*, their high priests, the omniscient ones, tell the Kogi that it is no longer worth it. The gods had given the 'younger brothers' the opportunity to build dangerous playthings such as cannons, helicopters, car, submarines and rockets, but the 'younger brothers' did not know how to handle them. So the playthings would soon set the world on fire and there was no point in their former activities, although the *Mama*, and all the Kogi people are convinced that they are the ones who will preserve and continue the human race after the holocaust.

I am the opposite of a prophet of world disaster. I am an optimist, because I still rely on the intelligence of the men who recognise and try to eliminate the danger into which we have manoeuvred ourselves. Later I found that the mam-Kogi prophecies tally with the traditions of other Indian tribes from Chile to Canada.

In January 1980 there was an Indian Congress in Montreal attended by Indian priests from many territories. The representative of the Yanomano Indians from Venezuela told the Congress (8):

In the vicinity of the country where my people live there are some mountains which are sacred to us. We call one of them the 'bear', another the 'monkey' and a third the 'bird'. Long before the white men came, our medicine men visited these mountains many times. No one else was allowed to visit this district. These mountains conceal great powers and the ancient sages of our people speak of dangerous material that lies there. Our tradition says that if these mountains were destroyed, terrible misfortune would befall. Massive rainfall would flood everything and wipe out our people.

Then the Yanomano had something incredible to say. A few years ago Japanese scientists had drilled in the sacred mountains ... and they found uranium!

How could this knowledge (confirmed two years ago) have found its way into ancient Indian tradition a thousand years and more ago; who knew that certain mountains concealed dangerous materials? Who could predict that exploitation of the sacred mountains would unleash terrible misfortune?

As the primeval Indians were certainly incapable of producing measuring instruments to locate the uranium, we must ask: where did they get their knowledge? was their unspoilt religious sensitivity enough to localise the dangerous radiation? Or did they see creatures suffering an agonising death in the vicinity of their sacred mountains? That is quite possible, for nature does not look after her uranium as carefully as modern nuclear power stations treat uranium waste. Nature makes no distinction between the living and the dead.

Yet even if we admit that the Indians had sensed the presence of dangerous matter in their mountains in some way or other, their foreknowledge of the latent danger involved in exploitation is incomprehensible. We are proud of the fact that our high technology has made the invisible measurable. But who handed on the precognition?

Who told the Yanomano about the danger hidden in the mountains? The Indians themselves supply the answer. It was their heavenly teachers!

Of course it is easy enough to dismiss the 'heavenly teachers' as figments of the imagination dreamed up by the primeval Indians, but that leads us into a complete cul-de-sac. Then we are implying that the narrators of all Indian tribes, and *mutatis mutandis* our biblical prophets, cheated and lied in their accounts of conversations with the heavenly ones.

A prophet like the biblical Enoch did not say that he had spoken to visions or travelled in the realms of fancy. Enoch makes it quite clear that he spoke to teachers who came from heaven and that they instructed him in his activities. So were Enoch, Moses, Gilgamesh, the Yanomano and Hopi Indians, the Dogon Negroes in Central Africa, the ancient Indian sages and the Kogi all lying? Are we dealing with a world-wide Mafia of imaginative storytellers?

The second 'solution' of misunderstood mythological messages and stone witnesses from the remote past by psychological interpretations founders on the hard facts which do not tolerate lengthy attempts to lay verbal smokescreens. Buritaca 200 exists. The cosmological model stems from an as yet unverifiable past. It had been in existence long before the white man occupied the terrain centuries ago and 'discovered' the Indians. They would have existed and continued to exist even if the white men had not scared them away and ill-treated them.

The way may be unpleasant and barely accessible to our scientists, but it is the only one that leads to the goal. The primordial teachers were extraterrestrials.

If we accept this (to me banal) fact, the whole history of

mankind would be brilliantly illuminated. It is high time to pull this wisdom tooth. It is high time to investigate the claims of the Kogi that their ancient priests had left in the temples 'memories' which more advanced men would understand. Perhaps the stone phalluses that rear up to heaven are symbols of the life that came 'from above'. Perhaps the 'genetic disc' is a pointer to the origin of the first life. Perhaps the engravings on the Tunja stones contain formulas giving information about the sojourn of the extraterrestrials. Perhaps the Archaeological Park at San Agustín is a gigantic memorial that was left behind – as a memory of the future.

Our blue planet affords an overpowering number of memories. What must happen before science finally takes notice of them? It will be too late after a global catastrophe. We can no longer afford to overlook warnings or ignore possible remedies.

We are not only responsible for what we do, but also for what we leave undone!   (Molière, 1622–73)

Picture Acknowledgements

The pictures on pages 2 to 7 were kindly put at my disposal by the Church of Jesus Christ of Latter-day Saints, Salt Lake City (USA)

Josef Blumrich: Page No. 19 (from *The Spaceships of Ezekiel*, Bantam Books, 1974)

Manfred Steinlechner: Indian ink drawings on pages 42, 50, 51, 61, 66, 142

Professor Jaime Gutierrez, Bogotá: Page Nos. 145–148

Patrick Utermann: Sketches page Nos. 184 and 185

Willi Dünnenberger: Page No. 187

All other illustrations are by the author

Bibliography

1 Legendary Times!
1. *The Book of Mormon*, 16th edn, 1966
2. HINCKLEY, Gordon B., *The Truth Re-established. Brief sketch of the History of the Church of Jesus Christ of Latter-day Saints*, 1978
3. BIN GORION, Micha Josef, *Die Sagen der Juden von der Urzeit*, Frankfurt, 1919
4. BURROWS, Millar, *More Light on the Dead Sea Scrolls*, London, 1958
5. WUTTKE, Gottfried, *Melchisedech, der Preisterkönig von Salem, Eine Studie zur Geschichte der Exegese*, Giessen, 1929
6. BONWETSCH, Nathanael G., *Die Bücher der Geheimnisse Henochs, Das sogenannte slawische Henochbuch*, Leipzig, 1927
7. *Die Heilige Schrift des Alten und des Neuen Testaments*, Stuttgart, 1972
8. HERTZBERG, H. W., 'The Melschisedek Traditions', *The Journal of the Palestine Oriental Society*, Vol. VIII, Jerusalem, 1928
9. LAMBERT, Wilfried G. and MILLARD, Alan Ralph, *Atrahasis, The Babylonian Story of the Flood*, Oxford, 1970
10. SITCHIN, Zecharia, *Der Zwölfte Planet*, Unterägeri bei Zug, 1979
11. BLUMRICH, Josef F., *The Spaceships of Ezekiel*, Bantam Books, 1974
12. HEYERDAHL, Thor, *Early Man and the Ocean*, Allen & Unwin, 1978
13. MADER, A. E., 'New Dolmen Finds in West Palestine', *The Journal of the Palestine Oriental Society*, Vol. VII, Jerusalem, 1927
14. BÄRWOLF, Adalbert, 'Radar entschleiert die Äcker de Maya', *Die Welt*, Hamburg, 6 September 1980

15. CORDAN, Wolfgang, *Das Buch des Rates Popol Vuh* — *Schöpfungsmythos und Wanderung der Quiché-Maya*, Düsseldorf, 1962

16. HASSLER, Gerd von, *Noahs Weg zum Amazonas*, Hamburg, 1976

17. HONORÉ, Pierre, *Ich fand den Weissen Gott*, Frankfurt, 1965

18. HAMMOND, Norman, 'The Earliest Maya', *Scientific American*, New York, March 1977

19. TALMAGE, James E., *The articles of faith. An Examination and Consideration of the Main Doctrines of the Church of Jesus Christ of Latter-day Saints*, Salt Lake City, undated

20. MAZAR, Benjamin, *Der Berg des Herrn* — *Neue Ausgrabungen in Jerusalem*, Bergisch Gladbach, 1979

2   In the Beginning Everything Was Different

1. MAZAR, Benjamin, *Der Berg des Herrn* — *Neue Ausgrabungen in Jerusalem*, Bergisch Gladbach, 1979

2. TELLO, Julio C., 'Discovery of the Chavín Culture in Peru', *American Antiquity*, Vol. IX, No. 1, Menasha, 1943

3. STINGL, Miloslav, *Die Inkas* — *Ahnen der 'Sonnensohne'*, Düsseldorf, 1978

4. KAUFFMAN DOIG, Federico, 'La cultura Chavín', *Las Grandes Civilizaciones del Antiguo Peru*, Tomo III, Lima, 1963

5. NACHTIGALL, Horst, *Die amerikanischen Megalithkulturen*, Berlin, 1958

6. DISSELHOFF, H. D., *Das Imperium der Inka*, Berlin, 1972

7. PÖRTNER, Rudolf and DAVIES, Nigel, *Alte Kulturen der Neuen Welt, Neue Erkenntnisse der Archäologie*, Düsseldorf, 1980

8. TRIMBORN, Hermann, *Das Alte Amerika*, Stuttgart, 1959

9. HUBER, Siegfried, *Im Reich der Inka*, Olten, 1976

10. KATZ, Friedrich, *The Ancient American Civilisations*, Weidenfeld & Nicolson, 1969

11. FRANZ, Heinrich G., 'Tiermaske und Mensch-Tier-

Verwandlung als Grundmotive der altamerikanischen Kunst', *Jahrbuch des Kunsthistorischen Instituts der Universität Graz*, 1975

12. WEDEMEYER, Inge von, *Sonnengott und Sonnenmenschen*, Tübingen, 1970

13. KRICKEBERG, Walter, *Altmexikanischen Kulturen*, Berlin, 1975

14. DISSELHOFF, H. D., *Alt-Amerika*, Baden-Baden, 1961

15. SÉJOURNÉ, Laurette, *Altamerikanische Kulturen*, Vol. 21, Frankfurt, 1971

16. WILLEY, Gordon R., 'The Early Great Styles and the Rise of the Pre-Columbian Civilisations', *American Anthroplogist*, Vol. 64. 1962

17. LOTHROP, Samuel K., *Essays in Pre-Columbian Art and Archaeology*, Harvard University Press, Cambridge, Mass., 1964

18. BENNETT, Wendell C., 'The North Highlands of Peru, Part 2, Excavations at Chavín de Huantar', *Anthropological Papers of the American Museum of Natural History*, Vol. 39, New York, 1944

19. EISSFELDT, Otto, *Einleitung in das Alte Testament*, Tübingen, 1964

20. BURCKHARDT, Georg, *Gilgamesh — Eine Erzählung aus dem alten Orient*, Insel Verlag, undated

21. WILLEY, Gordon R., 'The Chavín Problem', *Southwestern Journal of Anthropology*, Vol. 7, No. 2, Albuquerque, 1951

22. DAVIES, Nigel, *Voyagers to the New World — Fact or Fantasy*, Macmillan, 1979

23. BURLEIGH, Richard, 'Scientific Methods of Dating', *Cambridge Encyclopedia of Archaeology*, Cambridge University Press, 1980

24. COE, Michael D., 'Olmec and Chavín: Rejoinder to Lanning', *American Antiquity*, Vol. 29, No. 1, Salt Lake City, 1963

25. KANO, Chiaki, 'The origins of the Chavín culture', *Studies in Pre-Columbian Art and Archaeology*, No. 22, Washington, 1979

26. KUBLER, George, *The Art and Architecture of Ancient America*, Harmondsworth, 1979

27. BLUMRICH, Josef F., *Kasskara und die Sieben Welten*, Düsseldorf, 1979

General
MÖLLER, Gerd and Elfride, *Peru*, Pforzheim, 1976
MASON, Alden J., *The Ancient Cities of Peru*, Pelican, Edinburgh, 1957
MIDDENDORF, E. W., *Das Hochland von Peru*, Vol. III, Berlin, 1895
KRICKEBERG, Walter, *Pre-Columbian American Religions*, Weidenfeld & Nicolson, 1961
WAISBARD, Simone, *Die Kultur der Inkas*, Zurich, 1980
RAIMONDI, Antonio, *El Peru*, Vol. I, Lima, 1940

3   A Case for Heinrich Schliemann

1. BLUMRICH, Josef F., *The Spaceships of Ezekiel*, Bantam Books, 1974
2. LAING, Bernhard, *Ezechiel — Der Prophet und das Buch*, Darmstadt, 1981
3. KAUTZSCH, Emil, *Die Apokryphen und Pseudepigraphen des Alten Testaments*, Vol. II, Ch. 7, Das Leben Adams und Evas, Hildesheim, 1962
4. GRÜNWEDEL, Albert, *Mythologie des Buddhismus in Tibet und in der Mongolei*, Leipzig, 1900
5. BOPP, Franz, *Ardschuna's Reise zu Indra's Himmel*, Berlin, 1824
6. LINDBLOM, J., *Prophecy in Ancient Israel*, Oxford, 1962
7. KEEL, Othmar, *Zurück von den Sternen*, Fribourg, 1970
8. BEYERLEIN, W., *Herkunft und Geschichte der ältesten Sinai-Traditionen*, 1961
9. DUMMERMUTH, Fritz, Separatdruck der theologischen Fakultät der Universität Basel, *Theol. Zeitschrift*, No. 17, 1961 and No. 19, 1963
10. DUMMERMUTH, Fritz, 'Biblische Offenbarungsphänomene', *Theologische Zeitschrift*, No. 21, 1965
11. TORREY, C., *Pseudo-Ezekiel and the Original Prophecy*, New Haven, 1930
12. SMEND, Rudolf, *Der Prophet Ezechiel*, Leipzig, 1880

13. BAUMGARTNER, W., *Hebraisches Schulbuch*, 26th edn, Basle, 1971
14. EICHRODT, W., *Das Alte Testament deutsch — Der Prophet Hesekiel*, Göttingen, 1968
15. PRAGER, Mirjam and STEMBERGER, Günter, *Die Bibel*, Salzburg, 1976
16. RICHTER, G., 'Der ezechielsche Tempel — Eine exegetische Studie über Ezechiel', *Beiträge zur Förderung christlicher Theologie*, 16. Jahrgang, Heft 12, Tübingen, 1912
17. REUSS, Eduard D., *Das Alte Testament — die Propheten*, Vol. 2, Braunschweig, 1892
18. HAUCK, Albert D., *Realencyklopädie für Protestantische Theologie und Kirche*, Chap. Ezekiel, Graz, 1969
19. CHIPIEZ, Charles and PERROT, Georges, *Le temple de Jérusalem et la maison du Bois-Liban, Restitués d'après Ezéchiel et le livre des Rois*, Paris, 1889
20. THENIUS, Otto, *Die Bücher der Könige — Kurzgefasstes exegetisches Handbuch zum Alten Testament*, Leipzig, 1849

General
BRUGG, Elmar, *Tragik und schöpferischer Mensch*, Baden/ Switzerland, 1965
ZIMMERLI, Walther, *Ezechiel*, Vol. XIII/2, Neukirchen-Vluyn, 1969
BAUMANN, Eberhard D., 'Die Hauptvisionen Hesekiels', *Zeitschrift für die Alttestamentliche Wissenschaft*, Vol. 67, Berlin, 1956

4 The Strategy of the Gods

1. 'Indio-Kultur im Dschungel, *Der Spiegel*, 1 February 1981
2. STÖPEL, Theodor K., *Südamerikanische prähistorische Tempel und Gottheiten*, Frankfurt, 1912
3. PREUSS, Theodor K., *Monumentale vorgeschichliche Kunst*, Göttingen, 1929
4. NACHTIGALL, Horst, *Die Amerikanischen Megalithkulturen*, Berlin, 1958

5. SOTO, Alvaro, *San Agustín*, Instituto Colombiano de Antropología, Bogotá, undated
6. DISSELHOFF, H. D., 'Die Kunst der Andenländer', *Alt-Amerika — Die Hochkulturen der Alten Welt*, Baden-Baden, 1961
7. KAPP, Martin, 'Im finstern zwanzigsten Jahrhundert', *Information der Internationalen Treuhand AG*, Heft 64, 1981
8. NIEL, Fernand, *Auf den Spuren der Grossen Steine*, Munich, 1977
9. HITZ, Hans-Rudolf, *Als man noch Protokeltisch sprach, Versuch einer Entzifferung der Inschriften von Glozel*, Ettingen, 1982
10. THÜRKAUF, Max, *König Nobels Hofstaat*, Schaffhausen, 1981
11. PRIANA, Miguel, *El jeroglifico Chibcha*, Bogotá, 1924
12. RUZO, Daniel, *La historia fantastica de un descubrimiento*, Mexico City, 1974
13. 'Stinkbomben in Atomlagern', *Der Spiegel*, 1981/51
14. SIMON, Pedro, *Noticias historiales de las conquistas de tierra en las Indias occidentales*, Bogotá, 1882–90
15. NACHTINGALL, Horst, *Alt-Kolombien*, Berlin, 1961
16. PAUWELS, Louis and BERGIER, Jacques, *Aufbruch ins dritte Jahrtausend*, Bern, 1962

General
BRAY, Warwick, *El Dorado*, New York, 1974
BUCHANAN, D., 'A Preliminary Decipherment of the Glozel Inscriptions', *The Epigraphic Society*, Vol. IX, No. 226, San Diego, Ca., 1981
CRICK, Francis, *Life Itself, Its Origin and Nature*, London, 1981
CHAVES, Eduardo B., *Mensagem dos Deuses*, Lisbon, 1977
FRADIN, Emile, *Glozel et ma vie*, Paris, 1979
HORNICKEL, Ernst, *Sonne, Strand und sowieso — Von Inseln, Küsten und lockenden Wassern*, Stuttgart, 1975
HOYLE, Fred, *Diseases from Space*, London, 1979
HOYLE, Fred and WICKRAMASINGHE, N. C., *Evolution from Space*, London, 1981
POSADA OCHOA, Mario, *Gold Museum*, Bank of the Republic, Bogotá, 1968

5   The Eighth Wonder of the World

1. SOTO, Alvaro, *Buritaca 200* (Ciudad Peridida), Bogotá, undated.
2. BISCHOF, Henning, *Die spanisch-indianische Auseinandersetzung in der nördlichen Sierra Nevada de Santa Marta (1501–1600)*, Bonn, 1971
3. CASTELLANOS, Juan de, *Elegias de varones ilustres de Indias*, Madrid, 1914
4. PREUSS, Theodor Konrad, *Forschungsreise zu den Kágaba*, Vienna, 1926
5. KRICKEBERG, Walter and TRIMBORN, Hermann (and others), *Pre-Columbian American Religions*, Weidenfeld & Nicolson, 1961
6. REICHEL-DOLMATOFF, Gerardo, 'Die Kogi in Kolombien', *Bild der Völker*, Vol. 5, Wiesbaden, undated
7. REICHEL-DOLMATOFF, Gerardo, 'Templos Kogi — Introduccion al simbolismo y a la astronomía del espacio sagrado', *Revista Colombiana de Antropología*, Vol. XIX, Bogotá, 1975
8. 'Indianer prophezeien den Untergang des Weissen Mannes', *Weser-Kurier*, 21 January 1980

General
REICHEL-DOLMATOFF, Gerardo and Alicia, *The people of Aritama*, London, 1961
REICHEL-DOLMATOFF, Gerardo, *Colombia — Ancient Peoples and Places*, London, 1965
SOTO, Alvaro and CADAVID, Gilberto, 'Buritaca 200', *Revista Lampara*, Bogotá, No. 76, Vol. XVII, December 1979

Index

Ancient Astronaut Society
World Headquarters
1921 St Johns Avenue
Highland Park
Illinois 60035
USA
Telephone: (312) 432-6230

Dear Reader,
  Last but not least, may I introduce to you the Ancient Astronaut Society, abbreviated to AAS. It is a tax-exempt, non-profit membership society. It was founded in the USA in 1973. It now has members in more than 50 countries.
  The Society's objective is the collection, exchange and publication of evidence tending to support and confirm the following theories:

The earth received a visit from outer space in prehistoric times ... (or)
The present technical civilisation on our planet is not the first ... (or)
A combination of both theories.

  Membership of the AAS is open to everybody. A newsletter for members is published in English and German every two months. The AAS takes part in the organisation of expeditions and study journeys to archaeological and other sites of importance for the proof of the theory. A world congress takes place every year. Previous congresses were held in Chicago (1974), Zürich (1975), Crikvenica, Yugoslavia (1976), Rio de Janeiro (1977), Chicago (1978), Munich (1979), Auckland, New Zealand (1980), Vienna (1982).
  Please write directly to the Society for membership information and a free copy of the Society's newsletter *Ancient Skies*.

Most sincerely,
Erich von Däniken